little boy

little boy

Lawrence Ferlinghetti

FABER & FABER

First published in 2019
by Faber & Faber Ltd
Bloomsbury House
74–77 Great Russell Street
London WC1B 3DA

First published in the USA in 2019
by Doubleday, a division of
Penguin Random House LLC

Printed and bound by CPI Group (UK) Ltd, Croydon CR0 4YY

A CIP record for this book
is available from the British Library

ISBN 978–0–571–35102–2

10 9 8 7 6 5 4 3 2 1

for Julie and for Lorenzo

La vida es sueño.

—CALDERÓN DE LA BARCA

*L*ittle Boy was quite lost. He had no idea who he was or where he had come from. He was with Aunt Emilie whom he loved very much. She had taken him in swaddling clothes from his mother who already had four sons and could not handle a fifth born a few months after his father died of a heart attack. His brother Harry aged twelve found their father dead on the back cellar steps of their little house just north of Van Cortlandt Park, Manhattan. "Poor Mom, no money, Pop dead," wrote Harry years later. His mother, Clemence Albertine Mendes-Monsanto, was born in Providence, Rhode Island, to Sephardic parents who had immigrated from Saint Thomas, Virgin Islands, where the family had been established for a very long time as wealthy planters until a collapse of the sugar market in the late 1890s impoverished them. The family had originally fled the Inquisition in Spain and Portugal but didn't arrive in the New World in steerage with nothing but their clothes. They arrived with all their possessions in steamer trunks, including candelabras, gold, and jewels, and thus were able to set up as merchants and planters in Saint Thomas where they soon had a great house on a hill with wide verandas looking down on the center of the town, and a family album showed them in broad-brimmed hats and black string ties. Saint Thomas was a Danish crown colony until America snatched it early in the twentieth century, and the Monsantos had intermarried with the Danes as well as with French settlers, and there were many French relatives who visited and were visited in France. Clemence Albertine had a French mother of vague aristocratic origins, and she still spoke French. So it went that Clemence Albertine's uncle married Emilie from northern France, and thus it was that Emilie who had always wanted a child came and took the newborn Laurent from his distraught mother and bore him off to France by herself. Little Boy surmised many years later that her husband, Ludwig Monsanto, a professor of languages, and quite a bit older than Emilie, did not at his advanced age want to adopt a son, and thus left Emilie with little Laurent. And so it was that Tante Emilie took him back to her hometown near Strasbourg (the town near where the famous Captain Dreyfus was from) when he was perhaps two years old, and there they lived long enough for him to speak French before English, and his very first memory of existence was being held on a balcony above the

boulevard where a parade was going by, and someone
was waving his hand at the great parade with band
music wafting up and strains of the "Marseillaise"
echoing. And the next thing he remembered was that
they were back in New York in a big high-ceilinged
apartment on the Upper West Side overlooking the
Hudson and the Palisades across the great river and
steamboats hooting their whistles and Aunt Emilie and
Ludwig somehow back together again. He had a prickly
beard when he embraced Little Boy, and the sun shone
on them for a brief time until suddenly Uncle Ludwig
was not there anymore, and this time for good. So then
again it was himself and Aunt Emilie in the big elegant
flat, but not for long, because she had no money, and
soon a Health Department man came and took him
away to an orphanage in Chappaqua, New York,
because she had no money to buy him milk and the
man said Little Boy would develop rickets. And there
was much weeping when they took him away from
Emilie, and so it was he stayed in that orphanage, and
years later the only memory he had of it was having to
eat undercooked tapioca pudding the kids called Cat's
Eyes. Oh the time lost and no other memory of it, until
a year later Aunt Emilie came and got him, and it was
still the 1920s in America. And how he remembered
her back then. She wore cloche hats and had her hair
cut short like Louise Brooks and wore always the same
elegant dress in the 1920s style, with low-cut bosom

and a long string of beads, and scent of eau-de-cologne always about her. And of course it was not "always," except in Little Boy's memory, but it must have been her thread-bare elegance (well hidden in her elegant spoken French) that got her a position as French governess to the eighteen-year-old daughter of Anna Lawrence Bisland and Presley Eugene Bisland in Bronxville, New York, where they lived in an ivy-covered mansion not far from Sarah Lawrence College founded by Anna Lawrence's father. And so Aunt Emilie came and got him, and so began their life in a third-floor room near the attic where steamer trunks with Cunard Line stickers on them shared space with old saddles and ancient bric-a-brac. But Little Boy remembered especially the dinners every night in the formal dining room with the big-boned Dutch butler who also served as chauffeur and was not used to butlering and juggled the serving dishes, while Tante Emilie conversed in French with beautiful daughter Sally, and the parents at opposite ends of the long table chiming in from time to time, or at least Madame Bisland did, for it was stylish back then to speak French and make grand tours of the Continent, especially Paris, and Aunt Emilie no doubt charmed them until a few months later she must have charmed Presley Bisland a little too much for Madame Bisland, and suddenly Aunt Emilie was gone from that house, and they told Little Boy that Emilie had gone away on her day off and had just never come back. Now, inasmuch as the Bislands had had a baby boy named Lawrence who died in infancy, it seemed an act of divine providence that they had now been provided with another Lawrence. And so it went, and Little Boy went on with them in the late 1920s in that fine mansion in Lawrence Park West, Bronxville. But he was of school age by then and they first sent him off to boarding school at Riverdale Country School at Riverdale-on-Hudson of which Little Boy remembers nothing but a kind headmaster looking after him, the youngest boy in the school, and they had a summer camp in the Adirondacks where Little Boy learned to swim and tie knots and saw for the first time the great woods, the huge straight pines, the shimmering lakes, the hidden streams, and the light shining down on them, as in the first morning of the world. But this was all a brief idyll he would long remember, while between camp and school back at the mansion in Bronxville it was a very lonely life for Little Boy, with the nearest neighbor out of sight and no children of any age to play with, and there were only the grown-up Bislands who to Little Boy seemed very old, though perhaps they were only in their fifties, and he had a room in a wing of the house where great oaks leaned their branches over his windows, and the wind howled against the stone walls of the great house, but the wind was his companion in that room that seemed so distant

from the rest of the house. It was only at mealtime
when a dinner bell sounded that he descended to the
family table to sit between Presley and Anna Bisland
who talked to each other as if at a great distance. Now
to describe each of them was a task for a writer like
Charles Dickens, for indeed they were like Victorians
in every way, each such a unique character of another
age, at least to Little Boy. And Presley Eugene Bisland
had been born into a noble but impoverished family in
Natchez, Mississippi, a couple of decades after the
American Civil War in which they had lost all but their
great old mansion Mount Repose. And Presley was the
last son in a large family, and there was no inheritance
for him. So at age fifteen he took off to the West,
hoping to strike it rich in Gold Rush California. He
rode the Chisholm Trail on cattle drives, learned to
break horses, and worked his way west as a cowboy.
Somewhere in northern California he put his stake
into a promising gold mine, only to lose every cent of it
as the mine failed to pan out. Broke but still only
twenty, he made it to New York City where—through
his family's connections—he was soon hobnobbing with
rich distant cousins (everyone in the Old South being
related to everyone else) and was invited to many
parties on upper Park Avenue and Fifth Avenue. A
handsome man he was indeed, and although he had
only a lowly job in the Abbot Coin Counter Company,
he was much in demand among the debutantes of that

period, including the young Anna Lawrence whose
family had a mansion on upper Fifth Avenue. It was
there that a marriage was arranged (with or without
love one never knew) between the very handsome
well-spoken Presley and the plain but demure Anna
Lawrence. So then after a grand marriage they settled
in Bronxville, some twenty miles from the city. At that
time, Bronxville was little more than open country,
and Anna's father had bought up most of the acreage,
planning a model town, with fine houses designed for
artists and writers, its own water and electrical
systems, etc, all owned originally by the Lawrence
family. Into this fair enclave moved Presley and Anna
early in the twentieth century, and by the time Little
Boy showed up they were already along in years.
To Little Boy they were always very very old, too old
in fact for a young child to make any kind of contact.
But Little Boy did love Presley Bisland. He had a wit
about him that sparkled through the courtly
conversations with his wife, the stately old lady who
wore black Victorian gowns, always with a diamond
choker around her neck. Years later, when Little Boy
came to know the writings of Mark Twain, he realized
that Presley Bisland was cut out of the same cloth, with
the same satiric humor as Twain, the same southern
background, even the same way of dressing. Presley
had grown up in a household steeped in the classics,
and had learned Latin at an early age. His library at

Plashbourne (as their house was called) was full of
Greek and Roman classics, as well as more modern
writers like Lafcadio Hearn. The library was a small
comfortable room just off the dining room paneled in
dark oak, with heavy easy chairs and nooks for
reading. At the dinner table, Presley would address
Little Boy with questions like "Young man, you've
been to school—who was Telemachus?" or he would
recite old chestnuts like "Horatius at the Bridge,"
thundering out the rhymes, or "The Charge of the
Light Brigade," making Little Boy feel the flames of
the battle with "Into the valley of Death rode the six
hundred . . . Cannon to the right of them, cannon to
the left of them," and the great phrase "Someone had
blundered!" rang through the dinner-table air. Or he
would give Little Boy silver dollars to recite some
chestnut by heart at the table. And Anna Bisland
would fade from their presence and there was only the
gracious witty old man challenging the world. (Little
Boy didn't know but perhaps she was pure Republican
and he was Mark Twain), and if things ever seemed to
be headed toward an argument, he usually answered,
"Right or wrong, madam, you're right." She perhaps
believed in God, and he didn't. And when he was dying
he forbid any kind of clergy to enter the house, but she
snuck one in anyway, having a priest in an adjoining
room mumble the last rites and then being spirited out
the kitchen entrance. While all that Presley said was

"Out of the house tonight, dead or alive!" Years later, reading Tolstoy, the Grown Boy imagined Presley like Tolstoy leaving his death-bed for the train station . . . And many years later, Grown Boy realized how much he loved that man, and knew not how to express it. But he remembered how once in deep winter, with snow blanketing the formal gardens around the mansion, he happened to see the old man in his pajamas in the middle of the night stumbling out the front door into the deep snow and starting to stumble into the storm, and Little Boy running after him and bringing him back into the house, and the dear old man would have frozen to death out there if it hadn't been for Little Boy.

AND Grown Boy in later years would never forget how when he was barely six years old his own mother, Clemence Albertine, and two of his brothers, Harry and Clement, came to the Bisland house one summer afternoon but were not invited into the house itself but stood on the great lawn in front, while armchairs were brought out for Presley and Anna Bisland while Little Boy stood sort of between them all, and the question was put straight to Little Boy, which way did he want to go, stay with the Bislands or go with his own mother and his own brothers, and there was a great and timorous silence in the summer air between them, and Little Boy was totally at a loss as to what to say or do, since no one had discussed this with him

before and he did not remember ever having seen
these strangers who were his mother and brothers,
and he finally stuttered out, "Stay here," and that was
it, as his true mother and brothers just went away,
and he only half realizing at all what he had done,
his whole life decided in an instant, and he stayed on
there, as it were, "forever," and he never saw them
again until he was grown, oh, what could the little kid
know, what could the little kid know about "class" or
"class distinctions" in the 1920s in Bronxville, New
York, when his mother and brothers were not invited
into the big house, although many years later he did
remember being very shocked by that . . . And life went
on, and there were no children to play with in the great
mansion, the nearest house being a quarter mile away,
and his best friends were the old Italian hunchback
gardener who lived in a shack behind the garage and
smelled of garlic—and the Irish housekeeper Delia
Devine who had a sharp wit and a sharp tongue in her
head with an Irish brogue that could cut butter—and
the young Dutch chauffeur who drove the big Cadillac
and doubled as butler with his big rawboned hands
clumsy with the serving dishes—and the Swedish
cook Annie who didn't stomach any frivolity in her
domain. . . . And the house and all its inhabitants
never faded away in his memory . . . The moving finger
wrote and, having writ, moved on.

 AND the time came when they decided Little

Boy did need some company his own age and that
he should go to the Bronxville Public School which
was several miles away in the center of Bronxville,
so that Little Boy would have to be farmed out with
someone in town so that he could attend the public
school. And so it was arranged that he would be
boarded with a certain Zilla Larned Wilson, a widow
with one son of fifteen, who lived down by the railroad
tracks on Parkway Road (the only "poor" street in
town). And it was a shock for Little Boy to be suddenly
transplanted to a totally different level of life, from
the rich house to what seemed a poor house with
its back porch backed up fifteen feet from the track
where the New York Central Railroad thundered by in
the night, rattling the windows. And so began some
seven or eight years with the cold Widow Wilson and
her son Bill who became a big brother to Little Boy,
and there was also a ragged gang of kids to play or
battle with. And Little Boy had one fistfight with a
kid known as "snot-nosed Red Neer," and then there
formed a small gang of kids with whom Little Boy
played Robin Hood and his Merry Men in the wooded
park by the Bronx River Parkway, and they fished
for crayfish in the little Bronx River in the park, and
Little Boy wanted more than anything a buckskin suit
like Robin Hood's, and would have robbed a traveler
to get it (that's how rebels are born). While back at
the house on Parkway Road he slept on a cot on the

back porch with the trains rumbling by, and he got
up every morning at five to run a paper route with
Bill, and it took until seven to finish delivering the
papers, and then he had to tend a newsstand at the
train station, selling the *New York Herald Trib* and
the *Times* to the well-heeled commuters heading for
the City in their Chesterfield topcoats and fedoras or
derbies on their way to Wall Street. And then there was
just time to rush home, change clothes, eat a muffin,
and take off for school by 9 a.m. And life went on like
that for a full seven years, except that when he got to
twelve years old he was able to go to Boy Scout camp
for a month in upstate New York somewhere. And all
that time he never heard from the Bislands (although
they must have been paying his board). But by the
time he was going on fifteen, he was beginning to
get into trouble after school, running around with
small hoodlums shoplifting stuff and stashing it in
a cellar behind the stores, and Little Boy was caught
stealing pencils from the five-and-ten-cent store the
same week he made Eagle Scout, and the scoutmaster
had to come and get him and take him home for a
spanking, after which the cold widow decided he had
become too much for her to handle and called the
Bislands to come and get him, which they did, and so
began another totally different life in the saga of Boy
who was no longer little. Lonely was the word, and
looking back years later he realized that neither the

Widow Wilson nor the Bislands had ever given him a
hug or a kiss. Now school was out and summer came
on, with the Bislands taking him with them to their
summer lodge on Big Wolf Lake in the Adirondacks
where he did the chores and chopped wood and dug
in the sawdust of the icehouse for huge blocks of ice
that he split and carried into the kitchen icebox. And
there was a boathouse with rowboats and a sailing
canoe which he was allowed to take out by himself
on the lake, and many were the sunny hours he
spent learning to sail by himself, and it was the best
summer he ever had. In the main lodge there were
birchbark signs that read things like "Come when
you wish, go when you will, and do what you damn
please" though he knew quite well that he could not
do what he damn pleased, but another birchbark sign
proclaimed "Behold the Fisherman. He ariseth at
dawn and disturbeth the whole household and goes
forth full of hope and returneth late at night smelling
of strong drink and the truth is not in him," and he
was allowed to be a fisherman and caught lake trout
as the summer passed away and then the Bislands sent
him away to Mount Hermon School on the Connecticut
River one hundred miles west of Boston, where for the
first time he experienced real camaraderie with other
boys in the dorms. His first year he had a roommate
on the ground floor of an old dorm, and this roommate
was a senior and was from India. His name was Jim,

son of missionaries in India, born in India, and he
became big brother to the boy, and one day something
happened that awakened the boy to consciousness.
In old age he still remembered it. Jim had Small Boy
down on the floor, sitting on him astraddle. He was
gentle but he would not let Small Boy up until he
would admit that he could not prove he was alive and
that he was not dreaming, and Small Boy kept crying
"But I am alive, I am alive!" and Jim kept saying how
can you prove it, and Small Boy was crying and Jim
just kept sitting on him until he let him up. And life
went on in his first year at Mount Hermon School
on the Connecticut River, due west of Boston, and
almost three years later he did graduate and went on to
Chapel Hill and the University of North Carolina and
graduated from journalism school and went straight
into the U.S. Navy at the beginning of World War Two,
and commanded a navy subchaser in the Normandy
landings and went to the Pacific as navigator on an
attack transport and saw Nagasaki seven weeks after
the second bomb was dropped and saw the landscape
of hell and became an instant pacifist and was
discharged from the navy in Portland, Oregon, in the
fall of that year, and got his first job in NYC in the mail
room of *Time* magazine in the basement of the Time-
Life Building, Rockefeller Center, and quit after three
months and went to Columbia University graduate
school and got an MA in lit and went to the University

of Paris on the G.I. Bill and after three and a half years
got a doctorate and split for the States and "home."

AND Little Boy, grown up after an endless series
of confusions transplantations transformations
instigations fornications confessions prognostications
hallucinations consternations confabulations
collaborations revelations recognitions restitutions
reverberations misconceptions clarifications
elucidations simplifications idealizations aspirations
circumnavigations realizations radicalizations and
liberations, as Grown Boy came into his own voice and
let loose his word-hoard pent up within him:

IN this existential café on the left coast of this
country, watching reality pass by with a wild eye to
inscribe on my brainpan a tale of sound and fury
signifying everything beginning with Mahler's Sixth
Symphony and our world lost in the last movement
before the final thundering crash of creation the last
thunderous gasp and our civilization passed down
from the Greeks really all gone now down the drain
And shall we tally it up now and see what's left after
capitalism hits the fan But in any case now it's time
it's high tide time to try to make some sense or cents
of our little life on earth and is it not all a dumb
show a mummery a blindman's bluff a buffoon's antic
asininities with clowns in masks jumping over the
moon as in a Chagall painting or as if we each were
dropped out of a womb onto this earth so naked

and alone we come into this world and blind in our
courses, where do we wander and know not where we
go nor what we do, with no assigned destinies except to
transmit our elements into other forms, yes just put our
parts back into the pot and stir to keep the old pot-au-
feu going on the back of the stove of the sun . . .

    LIKE that pot I kept going in that two-room cave
I had as a student in Paris 89 rue de Vaugirard in
Montparnasse where I painted on the wall a line from
Edgar Allan Poe Thy naiad airs thy hyacinth hair hath
brought me home and that was my first place all to
myself and never mind it was a cave for twenty-nine
dollars a month or was it a year with a stand-up john up
a winding stair halfway to the first floor with footprints
in the concrete where you squatted and pulled the
chain and leaped out into the stairway before the water
came rushing down to flood the floor, and my front
room had one tiny window like a slot in the wall of the
Bastille looking out to a stone courtyard and I had a
single cold-water spigot over an ancient hollowed-out
brown stone probably there since the Middle Ages,
and there did I meet myself as if I were some sort
of stranger just come in off the still street lonesome
traveler with no naiad at all to keep me company oh
what a romantic illusion all that was but I loved it I
flung out into the grey light of Paris every day with
a hunger in my step down along the quays thinking
I was some sort of wild poet or artist, and I was

Apollinaire and I was Rimbaud and I was Baudelaire
and all the damned poets, the mad ones with the rage
to live, my collar turned up in the fall wind that swept
along the quays, I swept along too in the hordes of
brown brittle leaves (pestilence-stricken multitudes!) as
winter came down

   BORN into that generation that came of age during
World War Two and fought it, the "greatest generation,"
as it came to be dubbed, as it came to be remembered,
creating its own new world, and memory an hourglass
when you turn it over and all the sands of past life flow
down through it mixing recent grains of time with
earlier grains all haphazard together in the mix And
it's Rockabye Baby all the way down and on and on
Yes the "greatest generation" coming of age with the
absolute freedom and exhilaration of youth before life's
entanglements free to be a free spirit or a drudge an
angel or a demon a conformist or rebel

   AND I was never much of a rebel back then or now
but I was a part of that war generation born in 1919
just in time to join the navy just before Pearl Harbor
happened yes that was its birthing day December 7
1941 the "greatest generation" indeed born, they told
us, to make the world safe for democracy ha-ha but that
was no cynical slogan back then because we actually
believed it believed we were fighting the Good War
for an America that was full of hope full of amiable
optimism in a wide-open land still not all bought-and-

sold the last frontier still full of promiscuous promise
where the pursuit of happiness had not yet turned
into a rat race to corner the gelt of the world yes and
in 1945 when the war ended it was as if the whole
continent tilted westward and the whole population of
men and women who had been uprooted by the war
slid westward and the cry was still "Go West, young
man" as millions heeded the blind siren call unlimited
in a new age in which America and Americans were
triumphant so that so many people thought life was so
good in these States that there was no need for anyone
to rebel against anything which today would seem
impossible as when I asked a lefty radio host "Can you
imagine a time in this country when you would no
longer have to be a dissident?" and got no answer but a
wise smile

AND so where do we go from here, we of the
greatest genesis and wherein lies our greatness today
and are we all ingested by our omnivorous consumer
society our dominant TV military-industrial perplex
sometimes tending toward corporate fascism and
devil take the hind half of the world even though
even though the People (as in Carl Sandburg's *The
People, Yes*) still have not lost all of their hopefulness,
even though lost Jack Kerouac returning dissolute or
disillusioned from Mexico at the end of his Road lost
heart, and all the sociologists saying his tale was the
end of American innocence

SO did I come upon this earth with the astonished
eye of an awakened owl to speak my piece, while a
destiny that led the Italian and Portuguese to the
Americas is strange enough but one that leads from
Portugal to the Virgin Islands to Westchester County
New York and finally to San Francisco is touched by
the dark miracle of chance And let the dice fall where
they may as the seed of my mother's family blew away
from the rocky Monsanto mountains of Portugal
in some dark century out of the Inquisition and
landed in Saint Thomas, and all went down into the
twentieth century with some of the family migrating
to Providence Rhode Island a main Portuguese
port where my mother's parents put down roots and
then she herself Albertine later born in Bath Beach
by Coney Island New York toward the end of the
nineteenth century

O can you imagine Bath Beach way back then on
that sandy spot or island of American land before
Irish Coney Island became Coney Island with its
Ferris wheels and vaudeville hawkers and painted
dames astride tigers and other unrealities O say can
you see by the dawn's early blight And is our antihero
to be a luckless fellow and a superfluous man in the
New World or is he to lead a revolution indeed the
revolution of the downtrodden of the world against
his own country which was on the wrong side of the
people's demotic revolution or will he end with a lovely

wife with almond-butter smile and be beloved by all or
will he end in dark prisons despised by all who hate
revolution that might interrupt their hot pursuits of
happiness while we go on flittering away our lives in
our city existence on pavements far from the earth
beneath us and we on it oblivious of its turning

AND the small boy knows nothing, he is just a
part of it, unconscious in his little existence on the
turning earth in some town or city or yes and so he's
later handed off to a distant relative by an exhausted
bereaved mother who could not take on one more
child with her growing brood just after their father
my father had died And so was he bundled off in
swaddling clothes to a rural small town in northern
France and so did he see the great plough horses in the
rutted fields the hidden crickets singing and the birds
crying in the gathering dusk calling to each other or
to the unknown and the huge cows coming home late
from the fields herded by ancient warders with wooden
crooks the huge ancient cows lowing in some medieval
time with huge old cowbells each echoing their hollow
sound as distinctive as a brand upon them and the
ancient gnarled herders prodding the ancient beasts
with bestial cries as the red sun set withering among
the treetops and just before the light of the sky winked
out guardian angels spreading their wings from
horizon to horizon and night fell as if forever and stars
lit up one by one in the deep distances And so now

where away little American boy growing up speaking
French and what would he ever say to the world in
what language and to whom would he say it if indeed
he had anything to say or would he just sing it out to
the great unknown or might Little Boy be like a match
struck across a night sky lighting up the universe with
his laughter and genius or he could just be an echo
chamber an echo of everything that was ever writ or
said or sung still hanging in the eternal air the eternal
dialogue of philosophers fools and lovers and losers the
very tongue of the soul sounding through time And
is every newborn creature born pure and innocent or
a carrier of everything including all evil and so will
my little man be a born sinner or a radiant innocent
happy from birth an ecstatic singing creature oh will
he be the morning sun slanting through the trees or
just a new moon over Coney Island where his mother
met his Italian immigrant father driving a cardboard
automobile without a license in a bumper car on a
fun ride when their bumper cars ran into each other
long time ago oh yes it was a crash of at least two . . .
civilizations his mother a Sephardic-Portuguese-
French-American and his father a Lombard Italian
immigrant looking for a lady to have five sons oh
Clemence Albertine Mendes-Monsanto purely appeared
in a vision before him by Bath Beach Coney Island
in the French boardinghouse where she lived with
relatives The seabirds cried and cawed under cirrus

skies wild in the gloaming And then years later baby
cries like mantras in unknown languages in South
Yonkers a mile north of Van Cortlandt Park yes there
in a small back bedroom his brother heard his first
cry like a seabird maybe or a wailing, an ecstatic
sound of surprise to awake upon the bright earth in
New York, and what a scene it must have been indeed
this beginning in 1919 America as in Dos Passos' *1919*
or some other deconstruction or reconstruction of
history and kids in the dusk playing baseball in the
still country fields before the Manhattan skyline grew
up and the far shouts in the still air still echoing in
his ear when he was handed off in swaddling clothes
to Tante Emilie and carried off by her over the sea to
Normandie and then on into the heart of France saved
from the Krauts as they were called back then over
there over there and the Yanks coming and all that But
in the backward mirror he remembered Strasbourg in
the autumn of that year with the brittle leaves falling
from the chestnut trees along the boulevard with the
white mountains of Alsace in the far distance and a
military parade going by below the fifth-floor running
balcony of their apartment and someone holding him
in her arms and waving his hand for him at the passing
parade yes that was the snapshot he remembered and
then the shutter went off and there was dark again in
his memory and nothing more could he remember of
France and that far time except the sound of *tu* and

a woman's voice calling him *Lu-lu-Lulu où est-tu?* and
he was playing hide-and-seek under a chair and he
was Baby Lulu in a patch of sunlight under a table
with the wind outside blowing the leaves swept along
the street each a dead life in the autumn of that year
And the years like receding figures disappearing down
a long tunnel far ago and birds of memory cawing
and cawing against the coming night And then much
later along Riverside Drive with the Palisades across
the broad river in another year returned to New York
with Tante Emilie who had returned to her man with
Little Boy now speaking French but in America again
and her man was tall and dark and had a prickly
beard and was a professor of Hispanic languages
somewhere a shadowy figure who came and went and
then disappeared again for good from that big flat with
the high ceilings and the view of Riverside Drive and
the river with tugboats pushing barges and couples
strolling along a riverbank and a slow ship hooting
its horn in the channel below the Palisades and it
seemed to be always autumn although he and Tante
Emilie didn't stay there long after her man left for
good Oh the crying and the sobbing and the bathetic
fallen handkerchiefs and night coming then alone with
Tante Emilie and in the night every cat was black and
he was afraid of ants in the cupboard and ants grew
wings and flew in his face And there are ants even
under the Bodhi Tree with Siddhartha seeking light in

which he discovers the radiant spark at the center of
Nothingness
BUT I keep having the same dream over and over
always the same with a disembodied me wandering
around some huge city which after a few dreams
I recognize as Manhattan, yes, it's always Lower
Manhattan and I'm always trying to get back to
somewhere uptown or just north of the city like Van
Cortlandt Park over toward the Hudson and it's getting
later all the time and there seem to be fewer and fewer
buses or taxis or people on the streets as I keep walking
uptown through the gathering dusk hoping to come
across some subway station or bus stop or taxi stand
but I don't seem to be advancing anywhere as if I'm on
a moving treadmill always carrying me away as the
night keeps closing in on me far from some home place
WHILE that swart Bard of Avon summoned up
remembrance of things past and was echoed by Marcel
Proust in a triumph of backward thinking yes yes the
think-pad makes cowards of us all and time a river we
swim in freestyle and the past all mirage and the
future still to be dreamed up yes and *longtemps, je me*
suis couché à la bonne heure and yes I still go to bed
early and think think think mostly of myself the center
of my universe around which all constellations wing
and so am I just an old guy singing "Auld Lang Syne"
in a high drunken voice and reliving all his lives on
earth like Krapp in his Last Tape recording everything

he remembers or in the end Nothing because the older
he gets the more he forgets until in the end it's all
amnesia and he can remember nothing at all of vast
spaces of time and he's left only with his present
moment or everybody's present moment the great
terrible moving moment of Now alone with himself
and his lonely consciousness alone on his own little
island of me, and so is that it? Oh no not at all I'm no
old geezer with a squeaky voice I'm still a kid with his
memory intact projecting into the bright infinite future
growing up in the darkest and lightest of times on his
little island of Me yes Me-Me-Me that's all it is on and
on the consciousness of me of man on earth and it's
the Great Memory no end to it the silent dead march
the live march of time in consciousness Oh yes *je me
souviens* of course I remember I remember everything
about me-me-me and the rest of the world does not
exist Oh it's time it's time and time again And do we
have a plot does anyone does someone or everyone have
a plot if not a plot then a story line yes that's it
everybody every body has a line of me-me-me on and
on but this singular somebody is special yes most
special But anyway this is her story his story history in
a single individual a microcosm a solo being solo shot
one-of-a-kind here today gone tamale oh how the mind
raves on in its sensorium Scratch out not a line Once
it's said or thought it echoes in the air forever in
eternal limbo echoing on and on whatever Plato said

whatever Dante said whatever the guy-in-the-catbird-
seat said I heard it I hear it echoing down through
time corridors of time the eternal dialogue Yes Hello
hello Here we are again *mamma mia* the past still with
us still echoing and the future not futureless but
ordained by the wheeling Vico cycle of time and free
will nothing but a pollywog willing to lose its tail and
so with the arrival of the future each day each moment
newborn and not on a cycle yeah let me tell you Time
marches on in magazines and movies and you are
swept along in everybody's consciousness and I am
trying to put it to you straight in this precious moment
which is now the only now we know and as soon as we
know it it is gone into the great void past all things and
beings yes and is it paradise on earth or is hell other
people or does it matter what you call it Yes indeed it
does Your consciousness of it of him of her is all that
counts and you always wanting to feel your way into
her consciousness or his consciousness so that the two
shall be one the two consciousnesses merged together
and I am you oh yes that's it except what's this
loneliness that in the end always creeps in as if it was
indeed impossible to merge with another person
impossible to ever know that person from the inside or
to fulfill the other half of that person Plato's half
absurdly searching for its Other oh no It cannot be
done say the shrinks and yet and yet Do I not love thee
as myself phantom voyageur errant wanderer *flâneur*

des deux rives . . . mon semblable, —mon frère . . . but
still let us proceed as if we were still aboveground and
I am not Samuel Beckett nor was meant to be headed
always underground and his voice getting smaller and
smaller and more and more inaudible from Murphy to
Malone to the Unnamable gone mute gone deaf
underground Only one syllable left to utter and that
one unnamable unutterable final syllable the final
secret of existence of why we are here on earth or in
space in interspace lost afloat in the Internet or
wherever Only the music of the spheres in the end and
the rest is silence as Ham said over and over I am not
Prince Ham nor was meant to be Am an attendant lord
of the flies and I fly in the face of fate and why did she
cut the crotch off of all his underwears if not to de-ball
him It wasn't pretty that story in all the papers and the
helicopter flying over the scene of the crime along the
riverbank in the dark dusk by the Seine in another
century or early twentieth century when the Pathé
News cameraman caught the man in tails wearing
wings with a champagne glass in hand on the Tour
Eiffel and all his invited guests watching he had to go
they were all waiting for him to do it and he
plummeted straight down his wings catching no air
and plunk there he was a blotch on the sere ground
Lord save me I have only one life to live save me from
such vanity pull down pull down thy vanity old man
young man Let it all hang out but there are medieval

battlements in the way guarding the ramparts of self
yeah yeah loneliness where is thy sting I love to be
alone with my own thoughts my own filter that is my
own strainer to filter so-called reality that is what's
passing by the window as Creeley said about poetry you
should report more than what's passing by the window
said he meaning don't be so superficial dear poet
you've got eternity to dig among other profundities or
irrelevancies so I'll put another filter on my camera-eye
another lens for cinema verité up close and penetrate
the surface the surface nothing but ephemera froth on
the waves the sea's lips kissing the shore the sea's
tongues licking the shore panic ephemera and people
part of it and she let it all hang out and *elle avait des
tout petits tétons* sang collaborator Maurice Chevalier
during the Nazi occupation or was it someone singing
"Abie's Irish Rose" it's time gentlemen please hurry up
please it's time cyclical time on a bicycle or a
velocipede Let me not impede the cross-word traffic of
consciousness echoing around the world in a thousand
tongues and English the Latin of our days *le Latin de
nos jours* baby baby the language of the conquerors
just call it Globish and the World Bank running the
whole show into the ground Third World countries beat
down by loans by vulture capitalism masquerading as
democracy babybaby put your faith in us stick with
U.S. you'll be wearing diamonds six feet underground
De Beers on top of you in the deep shit *mamma mia*

and Thorstein Veblen drank the bitter drink alright
and have I not seen it all the long and the short and
the tall the dead and the beautiful over and over Oh
the mind of man and womban is a marvelous thing
and spring is like a perhaps hand stroking the
landscape of flesh and fowl and fauna funicular oh
yeah and everyman out for hisself and *sal si puedes*
everyman in his own auto everyman in his castle on
wheels autodidact who knows everything and his name
is Barney Google yeah lock him up Google him or her
or it and don't tell me all I read isn't true I saw it on
Facebook and the World Wide Web I saw it in the paper
I saw it on TV it must be true Don't call me Wiki
Wikipedia or Wikileakia I'm not wicked I'm innocent I
only want what I want so give me a good five-cent cigar
give me my sex-toy oh boy on and on will it ever end
endless the mad pursuit ah yes mad indeed of me-
me-me turtle-head turning every way and blinking
while the marble maidens on the Grecian urn pursue
each other still night and day my Anna Livia twinkle
toes But now we come to the broken sentences the plot
thickens and thins on earth or in the seventh ward in
Kearson Street or wherever she lies in bed with no one
or anyone Here is your plot your story line and I knew
her when she was Extra Virgin so the story goes
Gaudeamus igitur pull my daisy and I'll be born again
a new beginning sinning and singing trailing clouds of
glory do we come and paradise lies about us in our

infancy infantile as it may seem to Sartre and sister
Simone ask Algren what he sed about her a dirty thing
to say And I am obliged to lie down with fools said
another French dame giving head over heart and not at
all like you know who Miss Round Heels they called
her before she lost her looks and drowned in
Gloucester Harbor a long way from Beacon Hill but she
was fast on the uptake not for her to be ground down
by life no sir mister shrink she'd laugh you off the
stage this ain't vaudeville anymore we're into real life
and like with that other skittish Scottish-Irish lass with
the big eyes did I not stroke her hair one night and
much later she telling me I didn't know what was real
always looking over my shoulder for the greener fields
and the longer hair and the bigger tits my god it's true
every word of it in my auto in my Autogeddon speeding
headlong into the final endgame call it chaos

    BORN into such a world *balbutiant haletant
aspirant espérant* Where now Boy with your Tante
Emilie in her cloche hat a true 1920s flapper with the
long dress very décolleté on the fifth-floor running
balcony one morning the mountains the white
mountains of Alsace in the far distance Where now
ghost come back to your early beginnings the first
touchings in the first light the first imprints early
footprints handprints on the sands of me-me-me *je
me souviens* and I was hiding under a pillow and she
calling *Lu-Lu-Lulu où est-tu?* and she bent over me

décolleté Did I not glimpse full happiness then never
again the sun just turning the far corner beyond the
boulevard the sun shone in the chestnut trees the
breeze stirred them though all was silent Nothing
stirred the universe holding its breath the eternal
morning the first morning of the world in my little crib
on the French balcony when she bent over me her hair
straight like Louise Brooks curved around the ear
Did they call it a bob was it bobbed hair what did I
know primary imprint the sun echoing in the chestnut
trees *les marroniers* a voice beyond all time was calling
Aie! Aie!

A far cry a distant singing down to today echoing
do I not hear it still I hear Ti Jean Jack Kerouac
singing drunk Ti Jean whom Ginzy always tried to
make into a gay whereas Ti Jean was straight as they
come always chasing skirts before alcohol replaced
them Ti Jean built like a lumberjack in plaid shirts
and baseball cap you have seen the photos when later
he was blotto and bloated a sad story indeed and Ginzy
always going for straights whom he loved to convert
or at least tried and succeeded sometime suck-seeded
at least part-time with for instance Neal Cocksman
and Adonis poor sweet Allen not always so sweet yet
compassion his great thing he found in Buddhist
consciousness lovely Allen always falling in love with
straights like Peter whom he converted most of the
time at least oh what a tale signifying something by

the River Liffey and onward into the sea the sea the
great maw the final maw mother of us all father of
us all where we come from where we go from Sea sea
lapping forever on our shores on its shores lent to us
by the sea for this fleeting moment in eternity these
fair beaches those far reaches we roost upon but the
sea soon will take them back the icebergs melting and
all that and humankind the temporary tenant floating
toward the precipice unable to stop itself and its self-
destruction yes a civilization incapable of solving its
problems that are killing it is a decadent civilization
sed Aimé Césaire a civilization that chooses to close
its eyes to its most crucial problems is a moribund
civilization a civilization that lives by cunning and
fraud is a gone civilization or so you would think if you
thought at all if I thought at all I might get a glimpse
of it *la chute* the fall the failing the exhaustion of the
life force that makes the world go round and round one
civilization *épuisée foutue* and *au revoir mes enfants*
the dusk is coming the dark descending but all is not
lost no never all lost as long as Buck can get his pecker
up and eat his Mulligan stew no matter what with a
pint or two me dandies here's to you and here's to all
of us including me-me-me I'm still breathing I'm still
thinking tick-tick there's no blood running out not yet
at least while I can still put together a consciousness
of sorts becoming dumber and dumber day by day
Will I never learn the ways of the heart the ways of the

mind and which one leads the other oh I see said the
blind man who didn't see at all didn't see the sea And
a river ran through his life through my life a river runs
through it mysterious and wisterias while baboons
make good bedfellows and *tante-pis* Les Soldats de
l'Éternité now marching around the world through
various museums Londres Rome Vienna Paris copies
in bronze pants the original clay not fit to travel from
eleventh-century China and the great emperor Cin
who gave his name to China and began to build the
Great Wall in his free time which was infinite having
a million slaves to wash his undies with sperm spent
on a thousand courtesans and he Cin building his
vast tomb a microcosm of his vast kingdom complete
with thousands of soldiers and slaves cast in clay plus
courtiers and functionaries and servants and peasants
and commanders so that he Cin could rule forever
over his kingdom after he died aha alas all in vain! his
great tomb discovered by a dirt farmer in the twentieth
century and all then fallen under the rule of Mao Tse-
tung mouse-say-tongue and the Chinese Revolution
Mao say tongue-in-cheek ah yes many a year ago and
où sont les neiges d'antan? Romanticism is dead or is it
and I'm not one to tell in Hell there are no Frigidaires
and everyone laid out horizontal unable to climb out
Dante's fire escape with the tour guide Virgil And the
whole myth of Heaven and Hell a medieval superstition
an ignorant aboriginal construction inventing out of

whole cloth a hierarchy a kingdom of a make-believe
God invented to escape death-death-death imagining
an immortality a transmigration of souls and soul itself
an invention to perpetuate me-me-me And I saw God
and she was pissed by the Nazi Pope's fabrications O
Lord who told you you have a kingdom anyway for the
only Kingdom you have is the Kingdom of the Great
Unknown and all we really have is just you and me-
me-me in eternity as if eternity itself really existed oh I
resisted all that along with Jean-Paul Sartre and Being
and Nothingness take your choice How can you prove
you're alive how can you prove it's not all a dream that
everything you are being is not really dreaming as
Edgar Poe said it? just like that time when I was fifteen
and my first roommate at Mount Hermon School
west of Boston an older boy had me down on a rug in
our room and would not let me up until I admitted I
couldn't prove I wasn't dreaming everything and me-
me-me crying no no I'm real and you're real I'm real
but he wouldn't let me up he was big but he was gentle
he was Aristotle and Descartes he was a senior and
I'd still be lying there if he hadn't relented like a big
brother and not Little Brother Orwell for I was free in
the land of the pilgrims' pride America America before
nations were overrun with faceless hordes in search of
food and shelter circa 2184 A.D. in another age beyond
ours *après le déluge* where once the sweet birds sang
and may or may not sing again and Subcomandante

Marcos saying Please excuse the inconvenience but
this is a revolution

*BUT that old dream keeps coming back at me and
finds me always still walking in the great cement city
where now and then suddenly some stranger shows up
right in front of me like a guy with a flatbed truck who
is headed uptown and seems like he's willing to give
me a ride but just as sudden he vanishes in the dusk
and again there is no one in the street except me and I
keep walking and then just as suddenly a hay wagon
appears in front of me with a hayseed driver exhorting
his horses to move on but they won't move as he yells to
me to "hop on!" but the horses still don't move and the
whole scene fades away with me still on the pavement,
looking for home . . .*

GOD whose invisible proof may possibly exist
controls everything through the gates of the sun, all
life on earth day and night, night and day, light and
shadow, light and total darkness, And wasn't it clever
the way humans have dreamed up gods who can't be
seen invisible gods who hang out in some high place
Valhalla or Heaven and have strange names or Greek
names or no name at all but in any case can't be seen
or unseen and therefore can't be proved to not exist yes
indeed what a tall tale to tell over and over in temples
churches or sin-agogs or other far-out agogs or pulpits
made of metaphysics or Pataphysics or psychosomatic
syllogistics Lord Lord am I not my brother's keeper

DON'T hand me that all that blarney about we're
all in the same boat or the same bathtub and don't
throw out the baby with the bathing beauty hubba-
hubba so let's all now together stroke-stroke-stroke
I'm the cockswain and you're the peon rowing for
your life while the bare truth is that there ain't enuf
life jackets to go around especially since nobody will
stop having babies and it's every man for himself *sal si
puedes* over and over blam-blam and set 'em up in the
other alley and let's fuck fuck fuck for to fuck is to love
again but maybe we can go to the other side of the sun
someplace and start a new life a planetary civilization
a greater empire of a new benevolent colonialism with
us the benefactor spreading capitalism masquerading
as Christianity oh man beam me up Scotty there ain't
no intelligent life down here just millions of scrawny
humanoids like ayrabs or other assholes out to kill us
but we could use their mineral deposits gold in their
closets oil from the lamps of China or anywhere we
can get it steal it to keep our cozy cars rolling to keep
Autogeddon going and I ain't gonna get out of my auto
for anyone not even you dear god my car is my castle
and fuck you peasants the earth is flat in cyberspace
and we got the most powerful computers and most
overpowering armies so what's to stop us from
conquering the whole world flat or round We're the
victors we set the exchange rates the laws the treaties
not worth the paper they are printed on ha-ha we'll tell

you how to breathe all you fuckers trying to destroy
us bombing the Twin Towers you little creeps with
your pajama clothes and weird religions and who the
hell was Mohammed Zoroaster Sufi Buddha-boy Omar
Khayyam Rumi smoking hookahs and kicking back
we'll take care of you buddy after the Twin Towers
we'll generate this huge national paranoia allowing our
guv to abolish liberty in the land of the free with panic
legislation It's called shock treatment after any disaster
we move in and take over and South of the Border is
where we'd like to go with every dame every señora
that comes along with her promised land the vulva O
lay me down I love it aye mates to the breach the dawn
is coming and your señorita won't be blooming forever
So now where was I the original mail chauvinist pig
dancing on the rim of the world on the first and the
last frontier and all that Onward Christian Soldiers and
Love Thy Nabor only it's tough-love tough-tiddy and I
do love tiddies give me to suck and fuck I love you oh
yes and how many times in your life have you said I
love you how many times to how many people have you
said it how many times did Mister Proust say it when
they were doing their cattleya A voice beyond the earth
was calling and did the earth move for you whispered
that lover in the sack for whom the bell tolled as if
eternal love were only while the earth shook eternal
love only for a day and how long is eternity anyway if
you can see it in a grain of sand and it's always two

people in a pod and that's our story And I'll never
forget I'll never forget . . . what's-her-name what's-his-
name light of my life gay or straight oh how I loved
that asshole have I anything more to say I'm getting
dumber and dumber every day and when at last I
attain enlightenment I will know Nothing which is the
ultimate asininity while light is what it's all about light
makes Mary-go-round and all you can do is reach for
the brass ring as you whirl about around and around
ta-ta Don't tell me this is a wooden horse I'm on in a
circle of golden chariots with gilt horses caparisoned
with golden reins and riders leaning out to catch the
golden faux-golden ring and if someone catches one
another at once pops up to replace it just like consumer
society, *vero?* and I'm whirling about and the world
whirls with me the round earth that is not the faux flat
one on the world wide web yeah so is it the real round
man or the faux flat man who will rule the world in the
future in any future if there is one? oh what a question
as if there could be an answer and the dawn coming
up like thunder out of China 'cross the bay on the road
to Mandalay or Nirvana or samsara or paradise in a
spaghetti Western and John Wayne on his real horse
leading the charge over the far horizon over the last
frontier to the final shore and the white sand beaches
and the immigrants' dream come too true and lost
among the consumer-gatherers And everything's gone
straight to Hell since Sinatra played Juarez

BUT seize the night, she said, *carpe diem carpe notte,* Lay down lie down with me she said and it was a womb lost in time it's time for us to lie down together now you and me as if we were the first two people the first lovers the first man and woman or woman and woman or man and man for the first time in the dawn of the world and we're the first beasts the first humans to conceive of love beyond sex Yes she said first we must get beyond sex we must go through it yes and not because it is a chore no indeed it is a lovely thing a joy the first joy of all the ecstasy sweet singer hear my song and it is not a sin to lie nude together in innocence and ecstasy before the first preacher pasted the fig leaves on us although not upon all the other beasts of the forest the silent savages still on four legs oh no we were singled out to lose our innocence while the rest of the animal world was left to roam free of guilt free of gelt which soon crept into our special picture ah so here we are and let us lie down again as in the first light bend down bend down and kiss my body everywhere kiss my breasts my vulva kiss my penis over and over for I am you and I am every sex at once one on one the two of us are one sex one breathing body breathing love without even knowing what love is as if love were only bodies stuck together fill me with your love of me my body your body in me oh I am you indeed I feel it I am all of you and you are all of me and our eyes have it our eyes in each other's eyes as if to tell all to

reveal all as if two beings could ever be one could ever
really melt into each other absorbing all of the other
and becoming the Other and is that love is that the
ultimate lure only reached through the portal of bodies
afire only reached through those portals of desire
fellaheen *barbare* hairy beast I take you into me and
the earth shakes in me in us and this the male fantasy
and the female fantasy something else perhaps a final
charade between two bodies hungry for love beyond
bodies and Drive she said into the heart of being Drive
she said and be happy oh happy he or she who sights
the light of day dear light sweet light light of your eyes
light of my eyes Is there anything else that counts light
of our days the morning light early morning light that
pours in over the rooftops through the leaves of trees
through their lovely branches stretched to the rising
sun ah love let us be true to one another let us love one
another lover and lover brother and brother sister and
sister are we not all one in the early morn are we not
part of the landscape bathed by the sun of all our days
that falls equally on all yet as it falls creates its own
inequalities light and shade light and shadow ombre
and *lumière* deep shadow casting all in doubt casting
half of us into darkness making us dark making
us part of night the shadow of a man his negative a
photo-negative to develop in the photo-developer the
ambient solution of air and everything that surrounds
us war and peace holocausts and winds seas lapping

at the shores of our lives breathe in breathe out with
the universe the world turns breathing in the cosmos
green planet seen from space turning and turning
brown with the bad breath of machines Am I repeating
myself while with our computers we turn into plastic
machines of flesh and bone and how will the flat earth
look from outer space a round orb turning into noir
and us on it as on a lost ship in a Bermuda Triangle
all sails set and a smoking pipe on the captain's table
a half a bottle of cognac and the chronometer still
ticking tick-tick Let us go then you and me-me-me the
heroes and the heroines of this endless tale about to
end but I haven't even gotten into the story yet the
story of he-he she-she he-she-she-he me-me hidden
among the rest of humanity as if we were humane
whereas and wherefore we are maybe all insane and
the whole world a madhouse the earth the place the
rest of the universe has decided to put all the nutcases
that ever existed so that so that they would be isolated
and not spread their madness like a virus to all other
creatures sentient or not all over the rest of the cosmos
our crazy strain of genes propagating its own mad life
on earth

    AND are we really following some great
unconscious dictation a hidden force a life force
driving us all and not just us but all being sentient or
not and just what is it then this life force that drives
everything that leads everything and everyone and

if it leads then we must follow so that this leader is a
kind of tour director a dictator then but then who or
what's directing Him or Her and we're left looking
through the wrong end of the telescope with one leader
pointing to another leader diminishing in the distance
into infinity like the figure on the Quaker Oats box
showing a figure holding up a box upon which is a
figure holding up a box and so on over the horizon
with stick figures gesturing in the dusk and us still
back here on earth wondering what's driving us if not
this life force making every creature propagate and
propagate and reproduce himself or herself so that
so that we're back with me-me-me and are we free or
aren't we to fuck or not to fuck aye that's the rub the
eternal conundrum with or without a condom aye
that's the rubba-dub-dub and two in a tub floating out
to sea and yet and yet it's more than sex leading the
tune leading the dance it's not just ants-in-his-pants
because there's plants and other living things without
sex-toys who also all have the blind urge our blind
urge even when sex's saxophone is not playing there's
an urge to reach to grow to some light the light that is
the voice of the fourth person singular the voice that
light raises to express itself through the darkest ages
shining transcendent

   AND so into the crystal night of time, and the
most advanced astronomy, the most advanced science
is the most poetic, the very burning heart of poetry

as in Olbers' Paradox claiming that there might be a
place where all is light for with the naked eye we all
can see a few stars close up and the further away and
the deeper we look the more of them there are So that
in the deepest distances we see clusters and clusters
and whirling nebulae each one made of millions or
billions of stars so that in the infinite distances there
must be a place where all is light and the reason why
we still have night is that the light from that far place
where all is light simply hasn't got here yet and when
it does we'll have white nights with little black holes
where once were stars So that so that we ourselves
will be transformed into pure creatures of light whom
darkness could kill even as now I see a face that
darkness could kill in an instant a face as easily hurt
by laughter or light each a separate consciousness
a separate body whirling through air as the earth
whirls around and around each an isolate identity an
isolate inconsolable spirit body made of sea salt and
water and a beating heart and beating brain in each
in every body in our infinite courses stick figures
on the horizon a massed humanity of loneliness Oh
I would not want to dissect anyone as Flaubert did
Madame Bovary baring the very bones of her oh no I'd
rather keep the whole of her the pure person the pure
unbroken being oh such romanticism such romantic
illusion in an age of steel and smog and plastic and
what could I know of her in her *bottega oscura* oh

the dark workshops the *bottega oscura* in each of us
where poetry of self is born where heart's poetry first
generates in the hidden caves the dark bodegas of self
of me-me-me and you might remember the Roman
street named Botteghe Oscure where the Italian
Commie Party had its headquarters in Rome and a
famous lit mag was named after the street but not
the Party a great great mag financed by one Contessa
Caetani publishing far-out texts in many languages a
true international or supranational project And that *via*
was also the place where humpty-dumpty Commie fell
apart and destroyed the Revolution of the Sixties not so
long ago in Paris too where the CP barred the gates of
the car factory to the students writers anarchists dope
smokers psychedelic dreamers with love and flowers
oh yeah that was a laugh to the old Commies we'll
have none of that none of these sons and daughters
of the bourgeoisie looking for a new world ha-ha and
it's good night sweet prince all over again where all is
confusing and no one knows the answer to anything
or anyone for god's sake don't give me that again the
same old story of Adam biting Eve and down down
fall the apples of joy and no more *amore pane e vino*
and so begin again the broken sentences the stillborn
words the labyrinths and labyrêves of daily existence
and the parturition of the senses So sic transit over the
transom what-ho me hearties and where away now to
the four winds cast and a nor'easter blowing that time

in Gloucester in an imperfect storm So go below lay
down below batten down the hatches and let 'er blow
we'll be in Snug Harbor tight and dry and the mainsail
stowed we'll be in the firelit Amen Corner by the great
potbellied stove or in the swaying sack with me lady
ah laddie that's the way to lay low with language a
medium for communicating thought even on the high
seas of love Oh the world lies about us late and soon
like an endless ocean upon which ships flit like fireflies
and kingfishers dive and die and him with a stiff prick
all the time O lord teach us to sit still cried the Buddha
who had sat still on a mountaintop for a thousand
years holding a Vajra Lotus the very pulsing heart of
life And do I not hear the endless singing the music of
the spheres as some Greek poet heard it by the Aegean
long ago the high music of being the ecstatic music of
being and fuck the shrinks with their endless nattering
of malaise their endless digging up of buried bones
man do I need it do I have to exist side by side with all
these sickies telling me I am really sick etc etc I'll call
on those jerks when I need them maybe tomorrow and
in the meantime it's *amore pane e vino* back in the Old
Country where joy still lived and even ecstasy maybe
yes ecstasy and the sensual phosphorescence of youth

DID I say sensual or sexual no matter Aren't the
two the same only a difference of degree depending on
the temperature centigrade or Fahrenheit baby baby
keep your pecker in your pants stop panting and you'll

live longer and outlive your peenie-weenie that's what
the clap-doctor told Adam after a big night with Eve
back where they'd have us believe it all began ha-ha
I'm telling you it all began much earlier and Adam and
Eve were really bleached-out blacks where it all began
down there around the equator or below and so heave
away me hearties we're heading back to the tropics the
Tropics of Cancer or Capricorn or below so let her blow
we'll scud before the wind into our origins into our
destiny in the Third World War that is the War with
the Third World oh baby think that over and let out
your spinnaker and many the lad blown overboard in
the winds of sex and ecstasy into salt seas of tears the
wine-dark incarnadined seas as in that Turner painting
of the burning *Temeraire* and the world turning
noiseless on and on forever into eternity

BUT that old awful dream keeps haunting me
and coming back with me in the city streets walking
and walking with my collar turned up, except I have
no collar and no coat, as the winter dusk always
keeps falling in the cold cement city where lighted
houses whirl away over skyscrapers and disappear in
Siberia to the sound of sirens and it's like I'm that lone
woodblock figure in that black-and-white picture-novel
by Frans Masereel with its stark figure in blackest city
night, limbs lost among skyscrapers . . .

HUNG up on the cross the poor bastid just hanging
there on some rusty nails through the centuries an

orphan more or less his Father nowhere in sight and
his Mother a Virgin or an Extra Virgin as they say
on the olive oil labels a single mother for sure and
the sundown kid born in a manger rock-a-bye-baby
and how He happened to be born by Immaculate
Conception a tall tale if I ever hoid one oh Mary
Mother of God living in a convent somewhere or
maybe a serving maid in some monastery and when
she somehow got knocked up the monks or ordinary
guys or camel drivers one after another sed "Don't
blame me" and so then since no one would own up to
it the chief of the clan says Well then it musta been
some kinda immaculate conception or deception Yeah
man that musta been it And so it went into the books
into the holy books that is into the scriptures and
scrolls you betta believe it read it and weep and there
ain't no paintings or sculptures of a woman strung
up on a cross in the whole history of art there ain't
none except in the background of one hellish scene by
HerAnonymous Bosch and everyone knows he was the
leader of that secret sect of the cult of the Virgin and a
sex nut at that probably a whips-and-chains cocksman
who liked his women or men hung up if not well hung
And so maybe it shoulda been Mary hung up instead
of J.C. and Mary Magdalene in the wings also catching
hell from the sacred fathers for daring to dream of
being a liberated woman and so why not hang her up
too with the rest of the uppity dames but never mind

all that and we end up instead with the Son of God
on the Cross and so good night, sweet prince, into the
dark night of the soul climbing Mount Carmel with
Saint John of the Cross telling T. S. Eliot that in order
to arrive where you are you must go by a way you have
never been and arrive at last where you started and
recognize yourself for the first time And so with goofy
Vico we circle back to arrive at our own beginnings
and each of us not recognizing ourselves as a fourth
person singular or is it just another Protestant or
fish-eater mouthing the same old worn-out myths the
happy delusions with a made-up God who will save us
from total obliteration from absolute death on earth
the final annihilation of our little egos the total end
of our consciousness as we know it and consciousness
itself the only real god for all of us Yeah just think of
it isn't consciousness itself the ultimate god of all of us
for as long as consciousness lives we live and the only
other god that rules everything is great god Sun who
governs all life on earth so give great god Sun his due
and worship him as so many civilizations before us
did yes Sun is God and enough of that so let's forge on
through the night-mazes singing or coughing but at
the same time the ghost of the Holy Ghost still remains
the mystery the Holy Ghost that woozy dreamy third
leg of the tripartite government set up in the Kingdom
of God the Holy Ghost a weird mystical even non-
Christian member of that holy gang yeah that Holy

Ghost what is he or she doing in there with those old
Christies and where did he or she come from anyway
well look it up in your wicked wikipedias and you'll get
all sort of learned lunacies of where that mystic ghost
came from He or she comes out of the very roots of
existence He/She existed even before light yeah yeah
for in the beginning was the Holy Ghost and He/She
or It gave birth to our first light and so the Holy Ghost
is rather a nameless disembodied spirit an epiphany
upon the face of darkness and what is that or who is
that if it ain't none other than the Other that famous
Other that people like Antonin Artaud in Rodez
madhouses have been known to conceive shouting to
their jailors "I am the Other" and not just meaning the
other person in their cell considering themselves the
sane ones and everyone outside the asylum the really
crazy crazies and was it not Jean-Paul Sartre hisself
who had an epiphany and saw hisself as the Other and
started mumbling *Je est l'autre* or was it Rimbaud
the original true madman and some kind of junkie
telling us all we were the crazy ones and he the King
of Hearts so everybody else is the Other and all those
foreigners who don't speak our language all become
the Other and since they are totally different from us
and therefore unknowable they become the incarnate
enemy since the fear of the unknown creates enemies
everywhere and whole religions become enemies not
to mention nations or other nationalistic chimeras

dreamed up by nineteenth-century imperialists to
divide the world against itself for the profit of me-
me-me and the population of every tribe is swept by a
universal paranoia of fear of the Other man o man you
have it there in a nutshell or nuthouse and so on and
on and the good Knight of the Sad Face becomes your
enemy if not your enema to flush out evil or to flush
out good and so it's one two three what are we fighting
for? Lord save us and throw us a lifesaver from the
sinking ship of love

    AND it's our Last Hurrah and keep your pecker
up for if you outlive your pecker where does that leave
you like Henry from Brooklyn with the great gift of
gab who all his life kept it up and wrote great books
with it but then kept writing when his pecker couldn't
write anymore like an old fountain pen run dry oh
daddy call me a cab the dusk is yawning and field
mice squawk and run and hide from the rising tide
the icecaps melting and me-me-me in my kayak trying
to paddle over the horizon or maybe sailing into the
wind and blow blow thy winter wind mankind is so
unkind and manunkind populating the world while
the kingdom of beasts may or may not be different with
Rousseau painting *The Dream* a jungle scene with no
computers and no monkeys on cell phones typing like
mad and press the Save button to save us all on the
last frontier or the last island like Gauguin on Tahiti
having escaped civilization still trying to find the

final island because so far there had always been an
island further out in the archipelago as in Tahiti today
you're staying in the Tahiti Hilton and studying the
charts and thinking there must be an island further
out and so you go to Moorea which is further out but
there's a Club Med with golfing and tennis and fatsos
putting their balls even as you remember Mark Twain
or Mencken or someone said Anyone caught playing
golf should be banned from government yack-yack-
yack and there ain't no Jack in the Cracker Jackbox
anymore with Dylan singing the Jack of Hearts oh
happy days happy daze indeed so jump on your steed
and fly over the horizon And whatever you first see
over the horizon when at last you get there will be what
you want and long to love like Don Quixote yes he of
La Mancha on his faithful steed Rocinante as he saw
a highborn lady damsel who was in fact a whore in the
door of a hovel and not a fair lady in a great castle yes
Don Quixote saw a host of armed knights marching
toward him when in reality they were a herd of sheep
So you will see a splendorous Tree before thee yes the
very Tree of Laugh I mean the Tree of Life as it is
called in holy scriptures yes the very tree at the heart
of that famous garden where Adam and Eve did eat
much to their mutual indigestion yes the famous tree
whose leaves are tears or pearls depending on how
you look at them and the leaves dropping on you like
tears or tiny bursts of laughter while birds cry out oh

yes Let us prey or pray let us sing and dance about
that tree or lie down and lament beneath it as the
tears or pearls fall where you must watch out for the
serpent that snakes around the tree and whose scales
are separate sins and this snake none other than your
own sly pecker who hides his head most of the time
but sometimes when you least expect it rises up with
his one blind eye and straightens up and becomes
like an arrow ready to shoot into any flesh it sights
oh yes and off it shoots at whomever or whatever into
the unknown great darkness with the Knight of the
Sad Face and *The Divine Comedy* ain't no comedy
even though the soundtrack of the show has both a
laugh-track and a cry-track in the background and the
volume control in the hands of the producer but who
knows who he or she or it is or where hiding

Where in the pluriverse or in any other great verse
in which the where and why of the heart is in question
the location and state of the heart at the heart of every
other question the light that shines into the dark
abyss amen and awomen and ain't that the limit I'll
do a mudra to the Sun God the fourth person singular
personified in pure light and the Sun Word is light
itself as set forth by Sri Aurobindo himself or herself
if you believe in the transmigration of sexes for ain't
we all one as rabbits run and Sri Aurobindo and the
Mother are all one and the same person but in order to
arrive where you started you must still go by a way you

have never been So I'm a broken record or a human
tape-loop returning and returning with the same
yearning to be one with the Mother so sit still and
receive Her full in the face or in your tummy tucked in
and back straight in the full lotus position ha-ha as if
I'd ever waste my time like a leisure-class kid sitting all
day facing a wall and trying not to think and who has
the time or money to do that day after day and your
mantra is Let go Let go Let go of your ego Let go Let
go of desire Let go of your most precious possessions or
your dear sex organs nested together ready for the next
sex-drive an endless voyage to the lighthouse every
night

    AND so sitting in the Caffe Trieste San Francisco
where nothing ever changes decade after decade, the
faces change but it's the same characters drawn from
the population of the world, and where am I with
my constant companion my lonely self and the only
plot of this book of my life being my constant aging,
even as Pirate Jenny keeps singing I tell you I tell you
you must die you must die, and it's like waiting for
the other shoe to drop It's like waiting for God or
Godot who will never come but is bound to come
don't yawn I know you're still young and easy under
the apple boughs and it's a fine sunny day on earth so
why worry about who's making it spin and what do I
need a God for anyway when I've got me-me-me who'll
never die or like Beckett am I entering my monologue

stage like George Whitman in Paris aged almost a
hundred and the Last Time I Saw Paris I was with
Giacometti who made all those skinny anonymous
sculptures everyone called Universal when they were
really only anonymous and why didn't he do squishy
figures like Gert-rude Stein for aren't there just as
many fat men as skinny women etc etc but the fact
is most artists do figures most resembling their own
and you can imagine Giacometti never ate he was too
busy recreating himself in stick figures and Beckett
had a skinny consciousness too just like his writing
very skinny and shorn of accoutrements like flesh of
words writing just the bare bones as I saw him once
in the back of the Café Select 1948 bundled up in a
thin topcoat shivering in the Montparnasse winter and
himself looking like he hadn't eaten in a week like
he was still in the Resistance since this was before he
started *Waiting for Godot* and before it got famous
at the Théâtre de Poche or somewhere like that and
Beckett always like a shadow of himself like Giacometti
and T. S. Eliot in his wasted land as thin as Prufrock
with his trousers rolled and come to think of it like
William Seward Burroughs another Thin Man *el
hombre* invisible as he was called the old hip hustler
always ready to disappear should the fuzz show up He
was there but not there even when signing his books
in City Lights bookstore the original genius con-man

even later when he didn't need to be and was Clean if
you know what I mean He'd cleaned up as they say and
leading a straight life in Lawrence Kansas except for
what he might have been growing on "the back forty"
yeah he was clean as a shotgun barrel if you know
what I mean and you might say he wrote all of *Naked
Lunch* years before without ever eating it or breakfast
on the grass for that matter while shooting up in a
narrow room in that fleabag hotel in the Latin Quarter
and skinny Dr. Benway somewhere else also cooking
it up Sabbah Sabbah Sabbah Latah and that's the
skinny of it, the syllabus of the Skinny Lit tradition for
professors to micturate over with Don Quixote skinny
as his horse lost in the Sierra Morena lit up in a flash of
lightning in black of night

   BUT how now I remember a love as when I saw her
in Jermyn Street that time eating an apple and striding
along in a full flowered skirt, was it not a sight for wide
eyes to see and my eyes soared if not my heart oh what
a day it was the white clouds scudding in a deep sky
like sailboats or lost souls looking for a harbor and
later on the beach lying on the hot sand and the tide
rising, salt brine upon our lips, the dusk falling and
the gulls calling A cry beyond the world and long long
we lay in the sands, with lanterns on the waters far out
but then the final dense dark with no lyric escape and
the dawn never coming and nothing but night night

endless night the night of the great void in which the world spins and we upon it waiting for a strike of light to light us up

INDEED indeed I say mumbling to myself in the Caffe Trieste San Francisco, and is not capitalism the very enemy of democracy if you think about it or even if you don't think for the aims of one are the destroyers of the other and vice versa Oh but let's indulge in the Lyric Escape again and orgasms aren't necessary for ecstasy when there are myriad other highs to take us higher than parachutes as for instance as I remember Paris 1948 and the snow falling as I strode along through the Tuileries with my seabag over my shoulder looking a little like Conrad carrying Coleridge's albatross and the albatross my past I was eager to drown in this first time in Paris since childhood my second home come back again I felt like kissing the ground as when I landed in Normandy June 1944 but never made it to Paris until years later the sun shimmered on the chestnut trees and the snow falling silently silently on the tranced statues and the formal gardens and my life as a Sorbonne student stretched out before me and what is the plot of this novel if not the remembrance of things still not past for the past is but a cautious counselor of what has yet to come what has yet to transpire or expire so farewell final albatross as time ticks on and all of us like insects in an anthill seen from space all nebulous figures dancing in a

tropic night through the night-mazes singing a lyric
escape again then and why not Are we to live in
despair all the time thinking only of our certain deaths
so why not live the highs and ignore the lows Let
blasphemies rain down let tragedies and cataclysms
rain down upon us but we are not so easy to melt down
as even in death clowns laugh in our theaters of the
absurd in which a turd may turn into a toothsome
trollop male or female and what's to say you're wrong
except the medieval man in the round collar Amen oh
man om om as in the Buddhist chant the sound of the
universe turning yes the music of the spheres the
sightless singing a voice beyond the world the voice of
consciousness itself that higher or lower consciousness
they say that humans have and where did they get it
where did it come from if not from the great beyond
yes yes the voice of consciousness setting us apart from
other animals the disembodied voice of the fourth
person so singular the ventriloquized voice of some
god or goddess sounding in us And so faced into the
future or faced with the future my country tears of
thee Sweet Land of demi-democracy or plutocracy or
whatever you want to call it and will it continue as is
into the future or morph into something better or
worse in the course of inhuman events oh man Is
Rome burning Is Paris burning and am I signaling you
through the flames So Quo Vadis baby and where do
we go from here oh man and oh woman the two of you

will decide everything including your own ecological
meltdown as if mankind or manunkind were too stupid
and too greedy to save itself from melt-down eco-
disaster and so bye-bye civilization as we know it and
should I just let everybody else die as long as I got my
piece of prime cheese oh man it's all beyond me-me-me
and I'm resigning from the government to return to
private life and the Little Woman and kids as they say
You've heard the politicos mouth those phrases after
conning everybody around them So here we are again
dreaming of love in a hot climate Ah well am I raving
yes indeed I am It's the rage to live It's a rave a huge
high known as living a rave of living and breathing a
rave of loving and breathing and flying on Ecstasy that
drug of being of simply being alive It's a kind of
madness and am I mad or just crazy as Don Quixote de
la Mancha the chivalrous knight caught up in his own
illusions of saving ladies with his lance and unhorsing
rampant knights in iron suits with Brooks labels and
Yale locks upon the pants and with penis erectus for
spear he slays all old ladies making them young again
with a touch of his swaying sword retrouving them
their maidenhoods and -heads ah yes and why am I
still in this squirrel cage going round and round when
I want to be out in the green fields or on the high seas
with Greenpeace or Chris Columbus discovering a
symbolic India we have yet to find or even envision a
river still to be found in the heart of America with Jack

Kerouac and his merry band and not so merry as all
that in fact quite the opposite in their imagined quest
for you name it an America that no longer existed even
as he embarked to find it with his crazy crew oh and it
wasn't just America they were looking for driven as
they were by testosterone and the rage of living
personified by one Neal Cassady the driven driver of
their beat jalopy Cocksman and Adonis American
antihero outlaw cowboy who would stop to do brave
deeds and rescue a beautiful maiden as in all those old
cowboy shoot-'em-up Westerns only with Cassady his
hotrod was his horse and he gunned it over the horizon
but the only brave deeds he did were stealing cars in
which to screw the maidens etc etc his tale of
testosterone and a roving phallus goes on until he ends
high on uppers and down on downers walking along a
railroad track in the dark dawn of San Miguel de
Allende a lone lonely figure lying stretched on a
railroad trestle as anonymous as a stray dog in death a
fourth person singular and the Road ending with the
end of their crazy youth or the end of American
innocence as some weeping sociologists claimed oh
yeah wasn't that a sad story and Let It Come Down on
us yeah everything that the wiggy prophets prophesied
about what would come down on us in the last half of
the twentieth century when Moloch and Mammon
would take over totally and the Youth Revolt of the
1960s would be buried in the general conflagration of

greed greed greed and politicos selling us down the
river Lord Lord and yet new generations yet to spring
up to save us oh for sure let us dream For youth forever
sets forth again for the far shore to forge a new
conscience a new consciousness to become mariners of
love or avatars of love like certain gurus who love to
sleep with their acolytes or students and indeed why
not Isn't that the best way to transmit love pure or
impure or are those gurus just lecherous old cons or
whatever Oh no Everybody has his own calling and
some are called to Make Out as much as possible with
every possible Other and if I am an Other half forever
longing for the Other half of self to make my self
whole and why not spread Love instead of hate as if
Gandhi could stop Hitler oh don't give me that old saw
haw-haw but all I know is that Mount Analogue is a
symbolic mountain that doesn't exist on any map or
chart and yet exists for all of us to find and climb and
is it a mountain of love or a hill of hate and it's up to
you to decide and guide your life thereby or maybe it
isn't a fount of love or hate but rather just a metaphor
for absolute beauty or absolute truth or some other
absolute that exists though not on any map yes the idea
of truth and the idea of beauty still exist even if all the
beauty in the world has been destroyed the idea of
truth exists even if truth everywhere has been
destroyed as if there was not a single beautiful thing
left in a destroyed world old Plato said in his *Republic*

a platonic ideal as I knew it that time in Jermyn Street
or another time on the beach in Provincetown that
endless summer when the tide was out and along the
far strand there came toward me in the gloaming a tan
beauty with straight hair shining like a weapon in the
late sun and the sound of small waves lapping filled the
universe of sand and sky even as the rest of the world
was about to blow up or perhaps already had and this
moment on this strand was all that was left of being on
earth oh such romanticism you haven't heard in an age
but maybe isn't it about time for it For is science and
objective rational reason to rule unopposed forever
while poets and painters are all still trying to create
pure light the ultimate source and the first source of
life so why not a little bald romanticism in the face of
the dark cruel world in the face of the blind unfeeling
unthinking universe and blind fate with its scissors
cutting up all life including yours snip snip and you're
finished so lie down and die the earth turns on and
you are but an ash upon its wind so now flay me down
to sleep I pray my Lord my soul to keep which is the
grandest science fiction with Mozart's Requiem
echoing in Gothic vaults and *Dies Irae* descending like
fate itself upon us And all the time the Ouroboros
serpent eating its tail like life itself and by a process of
concatenous circumnavigation do we wind around to
our beginnings and recognize ourselves for the first
time like Ulysses returning home or Stephen Dedalus

turned into Finnagain where the iffey River Liffey
flows back to its beginnings only we do not begin again
our lives do not begin again but rather once flowed
into the sea there's no returning the all-engulfing sea
where we all began but even there we do go around
eaten by plankton digested by never-seen monsters of
the dark deep and then on and on eventually rising to
the surface of the seas in amphibious creepy-crawlers
and so creep up the beaches into the sunlight and raise
up new cities and new utopias with perfected humans
singing Happy Days Are Here Again and let the good
times roll over looking backward with Edward Bellamy
to our present day with all our fatal flaws in the
Shakespearean sense forcing us to fatal ends as life
itself cannot stop eating its tail Oh man can't I get off
this spinning meat-wheel animal kingdom oh man stop
the bus I want to get off And this the lament of the
disconsolate chimera in the wasted land of the world
unable to see beyond its dark horizon where light still
sings in the high voice of the fourth person singular
And yet we still have Night because the light from that
far place where all is light hasn't got here yet and we
can't go on like this but we do and there is no plot
there is only me-me-me and my Others and if Hell is
other people then that leaves me alone in Paradiso and
am I an angel or a devil dancing on the head of a penis
or a pin

    WHILE King Arthur turned into a crow croaked

in my window from his high perch telling me of the
endless life of the world as seen through his own
endless life and he cawed the great caw of it all even
as the universe remained a vast wheeling unknowable
thing with everything made up of identical particles
or seeds and some seeds were made of love and
some seeds made of hate and nobody yet could tell
which seed would in the end dominate the pluriverse
especially not in old-timey cities filled with fishermen
boozers layabouts dreamers liars seamstresses
salesmen con men porters politicians panhandlers
laundresses carpenters sausage-makers blacksmiths
wheelwrights and water sellers who went barefoot
and lived largely on bread and figs but also not in
megalopolises in future worlds in which nations as we
know them would no longer exist and the world swept
with multiethnic hordes seeking food and shelter
While still endless life goes on and will go on even in
the worst adversity and will go on with so many human
emotions so many lovers pining for each other so
many tears and so much singing and sighing so much
fighting and killing and so many flights of fancy and
flights of fear and so much camaraderie and solidarity
in spite of all in the face of total annihilation while all
the while in spite of all the slaying there are more and
more people overcrowding the earth because in spite of
all there is the chronic habit the chronic unstoppable
ungovernable urge to propagate with or without love

yes indeed it's the chronic problem of fornication that
rules over all governments as soon as night falls and
we are alone with each other in tight embrace ah yes
in tight embrace and here begins the real narrative
of me and you Tell me tell me before the dawn before
and before and before we were born before I was born
before the brave alliteration of language invaded
my brain I knew without words the rage to live the
hunger for living and the narrative of it still to be
discovered and articulated the narrative of living if not
its meaning since perhaps there is no meaning there
is only existing just as a poem or a painting does not
mean but Is and there are only episodes that don't add
up to any meaning but exert in themselves the pith of
living like that time when I was walking down a path
and met a shining someone or did not meet anyone or
was not walking but driving or flying and the earth
my oyster still as Our gang goes on killing the Other
gang on and on the rivers of blood still running and
where does all this end if not in our beginning over
and over Oh for a little erectile dysfunction before the
earth bursts its latitudinals with overpopulation the
spaceship earth overloaded and no end to the eternal
rutting and breeding a primeval instinct that will not
be denied and no politician dare touch it and don't
tell me I can't have a baby! is the universal cry and
the world a grand hotel where the lights are always on
and still every baby born between urine and feces and

every life an aperture through which the light of the
universe shines and every eye a precious lens saying
what can only be said in the voice of the fourth person
singular the wordless telling of the real lowdown on
life and what else is there to say what else am I to
mumble inside my monkey mind and so I'm still here
in this cave recording the shadows on the wall yes
recording all these reflections of reality or whatever is
going on and everything reflecting light and not-light
or life and not-life but who am I and what am I doing
here in the light and dark of the world and what do I
want in this world and if I can't answer such questions
could I just pack up and take off for some other world
where I would have to face the same conundrums as
if I had a bus transfer saying "Use for travel in any
direction until time expires" oh yeah as if I had a
choice and could go someplace else and keep avoiding
the basic question of what do I really want because
obviously I must want something am I not eternally
hungry for something like everybody else and mayhap
there are three kinds of desire not necessarily in this
order and not necessarily leading to each other and
they are the Desire to Possess and the Desire to Merge
and then the Desire to Withdraw and so then where am
I in all this desire and what did I ever really want or
what did I first want when I started off on my endless
adventures like what did the Man of La Mancha want
what did Ophelia want or Ulysses or Tristram Shandy

or King Arthur or the Rose of Tralee oh what did
they all want as I go on evading the question of what I
wanted when I first sprang up and I could just say like
Gregory Corso that I became a poet so that I could get
girls and maybe that's it after all and so then what is
the plot of this mellow-drama this melo-declamation
of my desire on earth and is it all a dumb play where
every character speaks and acts for no other reason
than to get what he wants and some hide it better than
others but it all boils down to no one but Me and so
Billy Boy here we are again and no matter where you
go there you are

    YES yes and he had lived and loved and won or lost
and he had wanted her and wanted her with her high
breasts and wild hair like a sibyl rising from the sea in
his illusion of her in her bathing trunks and bra that
time at that lake resort midsummer in the Catskills
and the heat upon them desire and flesh upon flesh in
the throbbing sun yet she still would not be possessed
and so on and on with desire and despair seated on a
bench in Central Park or under the linden trees in
Boston Common and the leaves falling that autumn in
the sea wind the brittle leaves swept along the brown
ground and our little hero is pure desire while despair
his other half is seated next to him in the fall of that
year when he was working as a waiter in Durgin Park
and hanging out in Jack Powers' Stone Soup Bookstore
and pursuing some other image of beauty and love as

he imagined it and there was the mad pursuit and even
then the possession on the backseat of a car but then
the withdrawal and the distancing and back he was
again seated on a bench and what is to be done about it
except to stride along the strand back in Gloucester
with *The Sun Also Rises* in one pocket and *Look
Homeward, Angel* in the other but his mind not on
books as the sun rises over the Three Pound Light,
and Vincent Ferrini the poetic conscience of Gloucester
comes sailing along with the wind blowing his cape
like a sail his wide hat held on with a string and
Vincent famous for his eternal flight and pursuit of the
eternal feminine looking always forward to new
conquests with greater sightings of truth beauty
goodness in a panting bosom and promises of
pneumatic bliss And he an orphan left without a tit as
a baby on a doorstep sprung up and ran into the world
chasing shadows of Mom and Pop in the suburbs oh it's
a breathless story told over and over in the history of
man and woman or woman and beast and the sun
setting on far pampas as animals stalk each other
including humans man after woman and vice versa or
twice worser or gender seeking gender tender in the
twilight and it's pretty basic ain't it if you know what I
mean and tender is the night or not so tender
depending on the avariciousness of hungers my god do
you have to lay that on me again yeah yeah well I'm
just reciting to you the story of me-me-me and my early

orphanhood and my life growing up not to mention the
inner terror of the worm in the bottle *mamma mia* the
worm in the bottle of tequila *reposada* a proof of its
100-proof power to turn you into a lusting lover lost
staggering-blind in the Mexican night or stoned on
mescal in a Mexican cantina like the consul in *Under
the Volcano* and *mescal Aficionados* laid out in dark
corners of the café called the Place Where You Lose
Your Soul where swinging doors let in nothing but
night and the horrors of the turning worm Aye but was
I not speaking of love as seen by Freud and his
discontents as if all comes down to sex as with our
little teenager chasing a girl under bleachers at the
high-school ball game and feeling for the first time a
certain surge in his body if not in his pants and her
elusiveness ending in nothing and the home team
routed to come another day boy oh boy the American
boy become a Boy Scout in the suburbs with merit
badges attesting to his expertise in knot-tying or
kindling a roaring fire by rubbing two sticks together
or two scouts together and hitchhiking his fourteen-
mile hike to win the country trophy for Scout Troop 2
and so on after living in an orphanage in Chappaqua
New York and forced to eat undercooked Cat's Eyes
tapioca It's good for your eyes they told him but didn't
tell him much else except brush your teeth and eat
your spinach and think of the starving Armenians and
it was the Great Depression and he delivering

newspapers at five in the morning to pay for his fodder
as well as peeping in early bedroom windows to
glimpse flesh on flesh in the dawn and sex the savior of
the working class strung out in bread lines until at last
when FDR and World War II bailed us out and he set
out to work himself through some provincial college
and henceforth emerged as a reasonably miseducated
product of high culture and not all so irrelevant as
rebels might imagine as if he knew any rebels anyway
since everyone really seemed to be in mad pursuit of
the same instant gratification and never mind rebellion
or the starving masses and so on with this abortive
attempt to find a plot in my life or in his life or
anybody's life as if there could possibly be any plot in
all of life as if anyone or any genius or any god or
goddess who had invented life could possibly have had
any plot in mind when he/she invented it what with the
blind force of physics ruling everything unthinkingly
unmorally nonethically Ah yes indeed I must revert
instead to the recounting and accounting of my own
fantasies my ideas and agitations and dumb
contemplations of the workings of the mind and heart
and as some love poet long ago said the heart has its
reasons the mind never comprehends oh yes indeed
but what is this organ of flesh known as the heart that
pumps blood with only so many beats for any one life
why is this involuntary muscle considered a guiding
force in the conduct of personal affairs while it is

known that the heart does not neurologically think
like the brain and so where does that leave me-me-me
filled with melancholy and confused imaginings in a
novel landscape filled with tragicomic adventures as
great as any in all the picaresque on-the-road novels of
the world with their heroes of sorrowful faces and mad
minds and hearts inflated with the rage to live And so
do I return to the monologue of my life seen as an
endless novel simply because I don't know how to end
any life So where away again my hearties once again
into the breach with breach buoys and breech cloths
covering groins male and female and we are not born
with road maps in the palms of our hands with Heart
lines and Life lines and direction signs at intersections
to tell us which way to direct our lives nor is there any
road map in the night skies or in the night heavens
with its Greek mythologies and pagan gods warring
with each other every night for our total mystification
and no one to tell us how to avoid black holes and
other life disasters even though navigators used to use
stars to steer by on the surface of the sea but not how
to navigate below the surface of living and how to steer
me down the street to a warm lover or other object of
my desire but listen let's not fall deep into romanticism
again for the warming world is too much with us late
and soon with the ongoing result of pure rampant
capitalism being the universal dispossession of whole
populations whose lands and natural resources are

taken from them by a new world elite a class above the rule of nations blah blah blah but the tide is turning and maybe some form of humanitarian socialism for the dispossessed will eventually emerge but unfortunately it might very well turn out to be a kind of state fascism oh yeah you bettah believe it brother yack yack yack do I have to listen to all this doomsday scenario by a bunch of weirdos and leftist creeps here in my cave with only the fourth person singular for company oh sure I know loneliness is my own fault and all I have to do is fling out to the nearest café or bookstore or movie house and mingle with the Jack and Jills who inhabit those places like they're all spin-offs from the 1960s when everyone was liberated to love it up with anybody and isn't that what everybody still wants and all of this would lead to universal peace where we could all lie around in saffron saris smoking aphrodisiacs stretched out with fetching beauties all of whom would be disposed to love me-me-me oh man do you dig it now or should we get lost in the unconscious machinery of the Oedipal conflict as it works itself out in me-me-me but why should I be afraid of Freud just because I was always in search of my father jousting through the world to find him while all the while unrequited passion unfulfilled longing drove others on including Sappho and Dante and Yeats and even he whose lady lamented his penis was too small Lord save us is that all that counts the

erect phallus still ruling all and the search for the
father nothing but a treasure hunt for Big Daddy with
the biggest bat in the lineup the kingpin in the
bowling alley of life so set 'em up in the other alley and
have another beer on the house great father great
artificer stand by me now in good stead as I set out now
to meet my fate in the forge of the world where the
plumber with the right joint wins the golden shower oh
fer Christ's sake what kind of highfalutin talk is that
let's get down to the mean streets again where my rebel
side starts showing up my shadow self my bad half my
dark self my wild half a real asshole my Other who
keeps on butting in on my life as if I needed him to
fulfill me oh sure and why not so let's get down to tin
tacks with this Other who is always acting up and
doing what I sometimes wanted to do but didn't have
the chops to do like he's some kind of swinging cat as
they used to say when it was hip to swing and hip to
rebel against everything O what a satire of himself was
he acting out his frustrations or convictions always Out
There doing what I could never do like getting drunk
and standing up in a bus and telling everybody to
"wake up and pee the world's on fire" etc etc a kind of
antihero I guess whom I could never be yet wanted to
be at least some of the time oh I'm sure you know the
type like Gregory Corso the poet always the crazy rebel
with his wild words which were right on the mark

pinning people down or destroying them with some
cruel truth so witty at the same time and Shelley his
hero oh I really admired him oh what is all this about
alienation from society or whatever and do we still
have to be alienated these days and isn't it possible to
create a society in which one would no longer have to
be dissident? Oh yeah well put that in your sebsi and
smoke it haven't I got better things to do being a big
pain in the butt always questioning everything and
disturbing everybody in their pursuit of property
which is what the founding fathers really had in mind
oh man give me a break just leave me alone to lead my
own private life but then other people come back at me
and say oh you and your ilk and your pursuit of
happiness intent on your own private gratifications in
spite of everything like even though there's always this
bully with his fascist mentality loping alongside of you
and if you just ignore this goon he will grow larger and
larger and take over while you're fucking around so
you have to turn aside from your private obsessions
and give this lout a few clouts to cut him down to size
or else or else and so on and so forth into the boring
workaday existence where everything is button-down
biz-biz-biz and no futzing around and no wild
imagination of another way to live or anything like
that yeah yeah am I still my brother's keeper and since
I have a lot of brothers am I to be the keeper of all of

them of all men and women Brother I ain't got a dime
And Brando on the take in *The Wild One* saying Well
whaddya got?

AND am I some ape sitting under a spare tree
waiting for the end or the beginning of the world in
some café still inscribing the amiable history of self
with mumblings and mouthings of various personal
assininities irrelevancies obscenities and obsessions on
and on to find the fucking universal in the particular
as they say as if the universe cared a damn what any
one atom thought or felt or spouted out of its mouth
or aperture front end or rear end like Paddy in a
corner in a pub babbling to himself or a fellow tippler
in the west of Ireland where Yeats is buried with his
outworn heart Under Ben Bulben and Maud Gonne
gone long ago after the Easter Rebellion alas poor
Yeats whose antique speech brash Ezra Pound tried
to make over much to the detriment of the Irisher's
lovely cadences as if all that had anything to do with
us that is you and me-me-me as we go on living and
breathing as if we would live forever as if time would
not kill us all in the end including our little ego which
we absolutely will not let die before us even though
Buddhists say we must let go of it if we are to reach
any sort of enlightenment oh sure Let it go Let it go
you don't need it and if everyone could kill their egos
there would be no need to kill each other and there
would be universal peace on earth yes indeed brother

blessed be the peacemakers and let us all chant om
om om instead of me-me-me if only we could if only
we would Let Go Let Go but I ain't going to let go
with Buddha and I ain't going to let go with no god
either even though the pope himself speaking Romano
with a German accent comes out on his high balcony
and urges me to Go with God since I ain't going no
place but right here on earth or in earth's sea and not
floating around on a cloud by the gates of some heaven
the exact location of which is ever more difficult to find
and the ultimate mysteries can never be discovered or
dissected or subjected to reason or to computer Twitter
which would ruin all the divine arguments and leave
only me to face only myself and look into the abyss
and hear in death the lyric voice of the fourth person
singular the voice of the lyric escape in which spring
every year travels north at fifteen miles per day and
wildflowers spring up in a wave across the landscape
at the same speed silently sending their crocus calls
for us passing in cars trains or buses at a much faster
speed in the wrong direction a blind life force driving
all of us animals and flowers reaching for the light
and birds calling in the chilly air a lyric escape the air
is bright with their calling as crimson sun cracks the
night and all is not lost though tempest-tossed and the
birds telling it over and over singing it to us as if the
world still belonged to them not us and there is always
and forever nothing but Now and past and future but

fantasies and the past a foreign country where they did
things differently but we are not sailors anymore not
able-bodied seamen anymore as we zoom across the
land enclosed in painted metal cans or fly through the
air in winged metal tubes totally disconnected from
nature as she used to be called but time that reviews
all things will certainly bring all down to earth again
for no one has yet been able to repeal the law of gravity
and even time must be subject to it as it is sucked down
the final funnel black hole even as earth the spinning
world itself in some not-so-distant future will be sucked
into the yawning maw of the universe even as the
pluriverse will be sucked down or up into some infinite
oblivion and so let us sing and dance on our tick of
eternity and its surreal narrative in which is embedded
the biography of bad boy me the would-be antihero the
virtual bullyboy born full of desire the omnivorous
hunger for life when he sprang up out of sperm into
endless adventures in that wilderness of being on earth
where there is only me-me-me in spite of billions of
other sentient beings four-legged or wingéd flying or
walking or swimming or crawling in sun or shadow
and prairie dogs sitting up and putting their paws
together facing the setting sun every day tomorrow and
tomorrow And there are no birds in yesterday's nests
and life goes on in that orphan's home at age six and
so began life with the dispossessed but still how did
Little Boy become so alienated in this endless tale of

endless thought and he always taking the outsider's
view when he grew up like he was Eugene Debs saying
while there is a soul in prison I am not free whereas
the straight me was like Little Lord Fauntleroy living
a straight life in luxurious settings etc etc with nary
a thought for his own unknown mother lost in transit
such a mixed-up story as is everybody's life And so it
was Little Lord Fauntleroy adopted out of that orphan's
home and no one throwing rose petals on him oh
does not everyone see life through a scrim a screen
between oneself and reality so that for instance being
an orphan boy still at ten years old our little hero sees
a Christmas pageant reenacted in a little town square
in suburban New York with Christmas carols oozing
through the snowy air and the Wise Guys coming onto
the scene in the make-believe manger and everyone
singing Christmas tunes and Baby Jesus in the manger
crying and wondering what is going on while all he
wants is his Mama and a warm tit and all he feels is
an immense lonesomeness on earth where he has just
arrived and which of us shall know his brother etc etc
and he alone in the empty universe empty of love and
warmth so that so that forever after he hated the sound
of Christmas carols "Joy to the World" and all that Oh
lonesome is a bad place to be crowded into with only
yourself And later he would wander in a wooded park
with his little band of school buddies seeing themselves
as Robin Hood's Merry Men and what he wanted more

than anything was a buckskin suit like Robin Hood oh he would have robbed a traveler to get it yes and that's how rebels are fomented.

YET even with such a fucked-up beginning, it was still "Welcome oh Life and let the dice fall where they may" as the seed of my mother's family blew away from the rocky mountains of Portugal in some dark century And I always dreaming a wanderer in some city an exile in my own land always struggling to get somewhere else to meet someone some shadowy nurturing being and always awakening without finding whoever yes this curious Little Boy who didn't know who he was or where he came from a kind of tabula rasa in a way and Tante Emilie had no money for milk and the Health Department came and took him away to the orphanage but after a very long year Tante Emilie came back for him for she had gotten a job as a French governess in a mansion in the suburbs on a hill in Lawrence Park west of Bronxville and they began living in a little room two floors up under the eaves of the grey stone house covered in ivy and surrounded by formal gardens and ate dinner in the formal dining room served by a Dutch butler who was also the chauffeur and Tante Emilie spoke only French to the eighteen-year-old daughter and this was in the 1920s before the Big Crash and in the summer of that year up under the eaves they slept side by side where a great oak tree leaned its branches over the gable of their

room and the wind swept the leaves against the
window at night but they were cozy inside and happy
then for a time a too-short time perhaps a half a year
but then the landscape grew darker the picture
darkened the film of her life went dark when Tante
Emilie disappeared overnight and just wasn't there
anymore and they told him she had gone out on her
day off and just never returned and must have been
(they said) a victim of amnesia and what else was he to
think or know the poor kid you'd say but ain't there
been plenty of other poor kids abandoned by mothers
or otherwise cast up alone someplace like Little Lord
Fauntleroy for instance which was indeed a book that
his Aunt Emily left with him in which a little
American boy inherits a fortune and a grand estate in
England and is spirited away by a "solicitor" for his
Lordship who wants the boy as his heir but doesn't
want the non-English mother whom his son had
married against his Lordship's will and so after the
son's untimely death the Lord sort of kidnapped Little
Lord Fauntleroy and the mother was not allowed to
come along and so the little tyke lonely by himself in a
great mansion like little me then proceeded to grow up
bereft of his dear aunt and how is it then that this
lonely lad grew up to be a part-time rebel Aye that's the
question for some shrink to explore or some behavioral
psychologist or barroom philosopher and it's two steps
forward and one step back to recover the past of

anyone as if anything could be recovered at all once
the moment of living is gone into the ravenous maw of
eternity even if you misspend a lifetime doing it like
poor Proust in search of lost time and what good did it
do him in the end in his cork-lined room in old Paris
breathing his last breath with a slight frown on his face
as if he had just missed recapturing his earliest
moment of waking life love lost and forlorn in the end
having never quite captured the love he'd imagined
and so into the great dark dark dark the interstellar
spaces where our dust blows we all go into it and who's
to say if we'll come out on the other side hardly the
Christians with their big book of fairy tales and is a
whole society to be founded on such fantasies such
visions but then why not? A vision is not to be
disregarded for without a vision to live by where are we
after all and so and so by all means let us have visions
and you have a vision and I have a vision and even
though all visions are myopic let us praise visions like
visions of a desert isle where there is absolutely no hate
or sin or violence and everyone's a lover male or female
and nobody has to work 'cause all the food is hanging
from the trees ready to eat or sprouting out of the
ground and all they have to do is make love all the
time if they can find it and there's the rub because it
doesn't grow on every bush like fruit no sirree you
don't find love just anywhere even in a perfect society
which is so perfect that dissidents don't any longer

have to be dissident and what are they all to do then to
occupy their lives and the consumer demand for love is
so great the consumption of love is so great that there
develops a great scarcity of it and what then what then
what with the population exploding as a result of all
that fertilization of love and it's an inborn instinct to
propagate the species it's a primal urge and every one
and every animal has this urge to do it over and over
and over with babies tumbling out of wombs or
pouches everywhere to satisfy that blind urge with or
without love and so there we are again with all the
others hunting love all the hunter-gatherers turned
into consumer-gatherers in a consumer society
consumed with consuming yeah turn on the TV and
git more out of it yeah git the baby outa the wombat
and plunk him/her in front of it in front of the big TV
and hook him/her into it for life so he/she will buy buy
buy and the boy growing up in such a society with
nothing to do but consume and be consumed by it wow
is that the end of it is that all there is to living on earth
but then again don't we run into that scarcity of love in
a world fighting for it and killing each other for it over
and over in endless wars oh ain't it about time to put
an end to it and find some other way to live on earth
yeah yeah some way between fascism and anarchism
oh man I'm tired of thinking about it so let's go out
into the fair fields and smell the flowers like Ferdinand
the Bull refusing to fight yes Ferdinand the true

pacifist the sacred bull with Buddha on his back and
everyone chanting om om om even with fear and
trembling and we can't go on but we do go on waiting
for some savior or destroyer or propagator or supreme
fucker beyond imagination and every sentence the last
sentence I'll ever write but then there's always another
thought to be spoken or written and we can't go on but
I do and I see I see cries the blind man who couldn't
see at all because he is seeing with his mind oh the
mind and its fascinations endless in its lonely
imagining and then also the fear and trembling yes
back to that every time between the laughter and the
high jinks and the singing into the night in drunken
taverns Oh we are poor little lambs who have lost our
way Bah-bah-bah Gentleman songsters off on a spree
gone from here to eterniteee and so on into the dark
night of the so-called soul with Saint John of the Cross
or whoever And Everyman I will go with thee and be
thy guide In thy most need to go by thy side to search
to find thine own true self and as Jorge Borges said
Whatever the destiny of man it in reality consists of a
single moment the solitary moment when man wakes
up to know forever who he is Ha-ha as if that were ever
possible for are we not each like an onion to be peeled
down to nothingness and what's to be found in
anyone's nothingness except Nothing like an empty
paper lantern hung in a leafless tree and all of
nothingness a big empty mirror capable of drawing

everything into itself like a vacuum and thus capturing
and containing everything that stands before it an
infinitely empty mirror this nothingness that takes
fleeting photos of everyone and everything passing by
so that so that we are all mirrors standing or hanging
around full of the echoes of each other reflected in
each other with distortions And so is not everything
that he writes here just scribblings on our own mirror
the mirror that each of us is and we cannot dictate who
will confront us and be absorbed into the mirror of
ourselves but what could a wandering lad on the
landscape of America know of all that as the many
yesterdays of history each a mirror lying horizontal in
graveyards, the Recoleta of race memory with marble
inscriptions in the certainties of dust and all our
mirror images withering away in a wind full of birds in
a lost El Dorado up an Amazon beyond which there is
no alphabet as still we go on searching like René
Daumal for a Mount Analogue not on any map and no
man is an Atlantis entire unto himself but today here
and now are we not farther from any paradise on earth
than ever before and has not the soul gone out of our
civilization with its electronic heart its very soul lost in
its electric pulse lost in the trash of its computer and
not a search engine that can find it and should we not
now rejoice over the coming end of industrial
civilization which is bad for earth and man yes indeed
the bad breath of machines is killing us even as we

speak and yes industrial civilization must go with all
its junk poisoning the earth and the Futurists were so
wrong imagining a *paradiso* on earth as a result of
wondrous machines early in the twentieth century
when they all began to hum almost as it were in unison
    AND looking back over the lost terrain, the great
misrememberer with myopic vision sees only himself
in the shorn landscape of half-overturned vehicles
of desire and misread signs at country crossroads
pointing different directions like Kerouac in Brittany
looking for his lost family with wooden signposts
pointing to tiny hamlets all beginning with KER- and
him getting drunker and drunker on native calvados
that Yanks used in their cigarette lighters in World War
Two oh poor Karook believing in Baby Jesus drunk
or sobered up wandering errant among the tangled
branches of his family tree like our boy looking for his
roots aye what a far-out search it was looking for lost
hearts and You Can't Go Home Again and all that no
matter how many roots you dig up no matter how much
he unearthed trying to reassemble it or piece together
some mute Stone Angel in his own Recoleta oh what's
to be salvaged from the shards and broken pieces of
marble with illegible inscriptions and a detached hand
pointing skyward while all the while he's growing up
into a culture of consumer-gatherers motivated mostly
by pure greed and why would he be attracted by the
ideal of an anarchist society with no place to call home

or wouldn't he have been better off seeking humanity
in new forms of art and so become a great artist and
the mind of man and the brute instinct mingled in
him ludic and ludicrous little man But the boy begins
with feelings and emotions and the mind weaves them
into his story his narrative and as we grow older our
softer parts grow harder and our hard parts softer and
our Inner Fish has the skeleton of a fish gasping on
the beach listening to Benny Goodman blowing on his
licorice stick in a big band and D. H. Lawrence holding
Aaron's phallic rod in his hand all reflected in the boy
growing up in old Manhattan full of all the adolescent
hungers and obsessions including the urge to waylay
the buxom wife next door thrice his age no matter a
breast is a breast wherever imagined in the mind of
an urchin on the night streets the heartless streets
the stone canyons with flashback memories cast upon
the mind-screen of the fourth person singular who is
your Other your inexpressible You who cannot be put
into words And so am I here regurgitating the sound
memory of my race my mind an echo chamber of
everything ever said or sung in the history of man
and/or woman or womban the incubator of mammal
life sweet singer in my ear echoing all sentient
beings in every tongue and tone while the Moving
Finger writes and having writ erases all of it with the
blackboard eraser of failing memory in an empty house
at nightfall by an abandoned pumping station on a dry

delta where still in the distance can be seen the bright
pulsing lights of a riverboat casino with its steamboat
whistle sending out cries of promised riches and naked
nudes wailing with lust calling out to a solitary figure
in the gloaming aye but still there must be in spite of
all a way forward through the morass of life and who
am I to say Pi is not God oh man just give us the dear
flesh to live and breathe in forever aye mates too long
at sea too long starved without the all-embracing
blind heat of warm flesh pulsing in the deep night
the libido itch in the crotch of love

    BUT far far from all that were we the night
before D-Day the night before that great assault on
the beaches of Normandy by the Allied forces yes
the night before at Plymouth with the deep country
lanes between hedgerows clogged with transport and
troops and loaded weapons carriers and thousands and
thousands of soldiers in battle gear all blacked out and
silent And in the whispering fields all around were
great encampments and whole armies bivouacked in
tents with small hooded cooking fires And it was the
night before Agincourt with the king visiting his men
around campfires in the muffled dark and then before
dawn the great movement started like a great beast
moving stealthily in the dark the loaded ships began
to move and to move out into the English Channel
And we were so young but didn't know it and we
were running a ship yes Executive Officer Lt. Eugene

Feinblatt USNR age twenty-four or -five was running
it and it was a great sea boat and could go through
anything before dawn June 6 1944 and we were
blacked out as part of a convoy-escort anti-submarine
screen steaming in formation east northeast in the
English Channel toward the beaches of Normandy
and we were thirty-three men and three officers on a
110-foot diesel-powered wooden-hulled subchaser at
5 a.m. on the blacked-out bridge of our little ship the
first light just cracking the black eastern horizon the
whole crew on deck at battle stations And in the very
first light on the horizon we were just beginning to
see a forest of masts rising up from below the horizon
with first just the tops of the masts and then the
hulls—a huge armada of thousands of great ships and
troop transports and escort vessels steaming together
from many separate ports converging with the first
light off the Normandy coast as we could hear waves
of Allied bombers going high over toward Utah and
Omaha Beaches shrouded in darkness and then the
distant explosions on the coast becoming a roar in
the darkness as we stood at our stations binoculars
trained on the French coast just coming into range in
the dawn light the armada steaming full speed dead
ahead for the beaches now And fair stood the wind for
France . . . Aye mates it's a far cry today from when we
sailed the high seas before the mast beating past Cape
Hatteras convoying ten-knot merchant ships in violent

storms and me in the crow's nest trying to see through
the whirling fog or crossing the Pacific on an attack
transport with ten thousand troops bound for Japan
or zigzagging across the Atlantic in a convoy of rusty
buckets and tin cans in a convoy of eighty-nine ships
only sixty-three reaching Murmansk yes the Murmansk
run in the dead of winter 1942–43 and the German
wolf-pack subs shadowing us for the kill Aye mi boy
it was a fine war I fought since I never fired a gun
except one burst of an antiaircraft Bofors at unseen
planes lost in the clouds ten thousand feet above the
Normandy beaches and later some depth charges that
went off too soon and cracked all the heads on our
own ship And that's it mates the greatest generation
fighting the Good War with the best of it spent on land
in London pubs during the buzz-bomb blackouts or
chasing the Scottish lassies around Loch Lomond after
grange hall dances while we was in dry dock up some
lock near Glasgow Rosneath it was and that's the way it
went and me enjoying every minute of it on sea or land
with the big war going bang-bang over the horizon
yeah and it's all legalized murder or state-sponsored
terrorism you better believe it Yet to tell the truth of
what really happened to meself on the high and low
seas I would just be peeling an onion to get down to
zero tolerance or the final skin of truth and then you'd
see me anew the true-blue me the eye at the center of
our little disturbance on earth the eye at the center

of consciousness and "the fly is where the eye was"
as Erik Bauersfeld's childhood friend said when he
came upon a fly eating out the eye of a dead fish cast
up upon a beach at night Oh the words that come at
midnight the night-soil of living and dying the sound
of the heart beating its thumping heard through flesh
as with an ear to the ground the sound of breathing
heard through a stethoscope the hope that all is
eternal and we'll live forever and ever if we are clever
enough to outwit somehow the grinning reaper with
the scythe ha-ha what an illusion what a farce when
we know for certain all the time that time will tell and
time will toll us under earth and the dearth and death
of all we love etc etc while we go astray in the hay and
what are ye going to do about it twisting and turning
to get off the hook and the tick-tock of time louder and
louder yes and so no help for it so why not have a gud
time instead with the Stoics and the Epicureans and
Lucretius and some Buddhists yes take off your skin
and dance around in your bones until you lease a place
forever in the sod of the turning world where landlord
never dies they say

    WHEREAS to gather from the air a live tradition as
Old Ez sed (and thereby promoted grave robbery as an
art form) a poetic technique upon which he jerry-built
his *Cantos* that couldn't possibly be sung And isn't it
all another way of listening for the eternal Ur-voice
the voice behind the voice of the race the voice of the

fourth person singular inexpressible ecstatic at once
coherent and incoherent sighing or babbling the voice
of all of us heard and unheard loud and soft just as if
there are only two kinds of poetry loud and soft and
two kinds of people hard and soft and some have hard
shells and some soft inside while the leaden wheel of
time measures out our lives in ticks as it whirs inside
its intricate watchworks with digital springs tick-tick-
tick around and around we go with Vico or Grandma
or little John or Baby Blue, and the glue sticking us all
together might be love or lust or hate or blood or you
name it whatever sticks you to your brother or lover or
Significant Other And so here we are again ok save us
from the Other, yet still I and my father are One son-of-
a-gun on the run along a riverbank along a riverrun
in sun or in deep shade under a bridge on the River
Liffey where I once slept a broke student imagining
myself Stephen Dedalus or mad Rimbaud and I was
Apollinaire and I was Baudelaire and I was Villon and
I was all the mad wandering tattered poets rolled into
one sleeping under the bridges of the world and later as
I was walking down Sackville Street or reading my way
through bookstores I met all the other great writers
and poets and great articulators of consciousness the
great grey Whitman arm in arm with Oscar Wilde
and Allen Ginsberg and Djuna Barnes crossing paths
with Shakespeare and Chekhov and Tolstoy and sexy

tragi-romantic Vincent Millay and Dylan Thomas sweet
singer of Swansea Dylan of all my days

   SO that measure of madness that moves life in wild
ways moved Little Boy away from couch-potato ease
and political somnolence inhabited by Mencken's
booboisie, for there are some people who just can't
stand normal life (but why be normal when you can be
happy?) and must always be itching to take off
somewhere or blow off somewhere and can't stand still
mentally or otherwise like as if they had an ant up
their blasthole or somewhere or they just have wild
imaginations that can't be tied up by conventions or
Ten Commandments so that so that the status quo has
always to be questioned and shook up or otherwise
disturbed in pursuit of happiness and property and I
was one of them, so ladies and gentlemen if you don't
want to be disturbed in such pursuits then you
wouldn't like my dear young upstart rebel or would-be
rebel or possible revolutionaire my shadow self but who
knows how he will turn out and will he ascend Mount
Olympus or Mount Disillusion or Mount Monologue or
Mount Analogue, and that's the question for any young
kid with his whole life laid out before him a bright
young kid with a great head on him and he could
become anything a president a great scientist or a great
holy man or a druggie or a bum or a great rebel for
there have been many heroes who were rebels yes so

many and bravo to all of them viva to all of them all those who overturned the apple cart to find the rotten apple before it spoiled the whole harvest and found the golden apples of Apuleius yes and there was a talking dog whose owner sold it because it wasn't saying what he wanted to hear and Italian papers reported their primal minister had a rectal dysfunction oh do they call that anal retentive and do they call him *il cavaliere coglione* and is not all of history a single parade with buffoons masquerading as statesmen and lamebrains and convenient idiots running the parade from beautiful capitol buildings and most all of them bought off by lobbyists before their first vote So what do you expect but universal fuckups and man too stupid and greedy to save himself from eco-catastrophe as the deep dusk falls Oh man there must be a better way to live and love and breathe Let's strike out for the future with fife and drum as in this poster by Levi's on street corners in San Francisco in the summer of 2009 that said "I am the new American pioneer looking forward never back No longer content to wait for better times . . . I will work for better times 'cause no one built this country in suits All I need is all I got Bruises heal Stink is good And apathy is death So with Old Walt I strike up for the New World A newer mightier world The one I will make to my liking For after the darkness comes the dawn There is a better tomorrow Look across the plains and mountains and see

America's eternal promise A promise of progress Go forth with me Go forth" And who was that speaking if not Whitman or every common man on earth or elsewhere who else if not an American certainly not a European with all his baggage of centuries like Pasolini said when he came to New York in the 1960s and met the New Left rads and wrote that he envied these Americans who could act without first having to wade through thirty centuries of intellectual baggage like what would Heidegger do or what would Descartes do or what would Plato say or Plutarch or Herodotus or Gramsci or some other great looming intellect haunting their old Euro heads yeah you can imagine what with the European Communist parties tied up in knots and eventually destroying the student revolution or revelation of 1968 And what Tarquin said in his garden with the poppy blooms was understood by the son but not by the messenger and so today the messenger embodied now as the media spreads confusion and doubt as to any eternal verity as indeed so do the philosophers or other heavy-headed thinkers who spread doubt in every direction even as Socrates did So that so that today there is a veritable clearance sale of ideas strained through the semiliterate media which ends up giving us a kind of Gazpacho Expressionism or cut-up consciousness as in William Burroughs' *Naked Lunch* or in John Cage's cut-up of any classic text as he did *Finnegans Wake* annihilating

the beautiful hushed talk of Irish washerwomen
gossiping in the gloaming while doing their washing
on a riverbank where field mice squawk and dusk
falling and night descending into doubt and despair
and fear and trembling O lord save us Blind in our
courses we know not what we do or where we go O the
semiconscious existential despair of not knowing who
we are and the boy all his life looking for himself and
for where he came from Father lost Mother in a
madhouse and he the little kid wandering around
knowing nothing having been told nothing of where he
came from and who was to tell him the little kid
plunked down on earth somewhere alone like a stray
cat or pup without a collar or name tag and how was he
to find himself in this twirling world spinning to the
music of the spheres which is the sound of Om in
which all sound is absorbed in which all thought all
feeling all senses are absorbed yes and Om the sound
of living itself the great Om of all our breathing the
voice of life the voice of our buried life the voice of the
voice of the blood then coursing through us through
even the penis that strange appendage a peninsula of
sorts a third arm or leg that so imperiously asserts its
authority and inopportunely rises up and inserts itself
into affairs personal or worldly and then so arrogantly
lets us down at critical moments at the very gates of
paradise or Nirvana or hell and refuses all our
incitements "of mind and hand" as some Frenchie

philosophe said even as he let down his pants in the
queen's chamber indeed indeed and we are left with
the perpetual astonishment of man on earth when
confronted with himself or his penis indeed what a
piece of work is man and this his daybook his
nightbook and I am not writing some kind of *Notes
from the Underground* as if I had any idea where any
underground is these days if I ever knew since I've
always been off in my own burb in some suburb of
consciousness dreaming away or otherwise goofing off
or picking my nose in hopeless cellars with fellow
travelers or their ilk imagining I'm going to change the
world or something and so I'm just some kind of
literary freak and my mind the constipated thought of
the race all too shallow to be called nihilism while all
the while all I want to do is walk around the earth
cooking the Joy soup What else is there to do with the
rest of eternity and would you tell me what it is we're
all supposed to do on earth anyway I mean truly just
sit right down and think of an answer to all that while
there's still time just give me a concrete answer as to
what humans are supposed to do with all our time
what on earth that is are we just to sit around like
blobs of perspiring protoplasm or like chimps in trees
scratching our fleas or whatever I mean maybe in fact
it's just dreaming that we're supposed to do after
everyone is fed after all is said and done oh no that's
just a big evasion of the basic burning question What I

want to know is what in hell are we here on earth for
anyway baby baby Am I your bedroom philosopher or
Doctor of Alienation Am I a willing well-fed participant
and protagonist in our consumer society a consumer-
gatherer or a rebel antagonist revolutionary an enemy
of the state or something in between neither fish nor
fouling-piece Tell me tell me the night is young and
you're so beautiful pardon me if I am overdutiful
Babeee and that's what he was asking himself as he
grew up into something new and strange at least in the
eyes of some totally objective journalist sent down here
to earth by some managing editor with a low tolerance
for malarkey who wants the truth and nothing but the
truth so let 'em have it tell us what is what and who we
are and what we are doing down here anyway The
top-dog editor wants to know the straight story and are
you man enough to tell it or are you brain enough to
tell it and are you man enough to say I love you man

   EGAD me hearties has it all come down to this,
sitting in some café (and cafés the habitation of all
lonely people) while most of the country is imbeciles in
neckties and I wuz one of them it's obvious or else who
would blather like this mindless as a mule with a sense
of humor or a donkey that brays every time he opens
his big mouth and out comes a bellow of a laugh very
derisive of everything on earth Yahoo! like he finds
existence a big hoot and a puzzlement to all especially
himself but after all he's somebody and was on the Ark

and all that which was like the first *Mayflower* landing
on our shores Well it all ain't that funny this long mad
history of man and mule on earth the flip-flops of
minds and behinds intertwined and how long can this
go on and is there a big ball of fire headed this way
And so it's Gertie on the grass alas and all of us sitting
there with our bare faces hanging out revealing all of
us as we truly are naked bodies and souls in the
paved-over garden of the world So take a close look at
us humans and humanoids chimps and chumps and
champs in a Saint Vitus Dance oh it's a samba a
cucaracha a mad waltz a taxi dance in the Roseland
Ballroom a madcap celebration of the coming end of
industrial civilization which is bad for earth and man
with the bad breath of machines inhaled by all and the
halitosis of greed perfuming our breath and Homo Sap
too stupid and too greedy to save himself from eco-
oblivion oh man ain't it Awesome! Oh so you think so,
you creep you asshole-first-class another one of those
crazies always against everything Well let me tell you
we've got you on our special list of suspects don't worry
we'll take care of you Better that you just stick to your
knitting or whatever you do to diddle yourself if you
know what I mean bye now and Have a Nice Day as the
San Francisco figurative school of painters used to say
blowing booze in jam sessions up around the Art
Institute while down Columbus Avenue just a few
blocks away a pickup band of grungy wild-ass poets

was fomenting a new counterculture a true critique of Moloch American consumer capitalism while the figurative painters kept fiddling their bourgeois tunes oh boy have you heard this before It's an old story Let's move on Don't we have better fish to frig Am I my brother's keeper still or was I ever my brother's subconscious which is a city built upon another city built upon another buried city back through unrecorded time city upon city buried layers of thinking and only the top level visible or audible so that so that history becomes a mirror with infinite depth layer upon layer of buried cities of consciousness and you and your consciousness just the surface image in front of a quicksilver mirror a Memory Chalet or is it just drifting water over the mirror of the past Cityful passing away Pyramids in sand Houses streets lampposts terminals tunnels blocks of apartments Landlord never dies sed Jimmy Joyce And our minds drifting away in dreams hallucinations visions of lovers on riverbanks man on woman man on man woman on woman on and on and all their voices commingling sounds of humanity echoing down through the centuries yes yes visions omens ecstasies and Allen Ginzy wailing "gone down the American river! Dreams! adorations! illuminations! religions! the whole boatload of sensitive bullshit! Breakthroughs! over the river! flips and crucifixions! gone down the flood! Highs! Epiphanies! Despairs! Ten years' animal

screams and suicides! Minds! New loves! Mad
generation! down on the rocks of Time!" Skin books
Parchment bodies Palimpsests of consciousness
Continuous epiphanies and moments of nudity when
the red sun sets on us stripped naked on the beach
waving genitals and manuscripts disappearing over the
horizon Goodbye! Goodbye! our minds blink shut but
consciousness continues echoing forever through time
though all bodies be gone And every word my last word
Nothing resolved Nothing brought to any conclusion
the plot left hanging the hero left longing for some way
up or out for some resolution revelation revolution So
where away then out of the playpen to the final
calamitous enunciation annunciation denunciation in
the Womb of the Unknown Word the baby's rattle in
this mumble And this ain't no novel but a kind of
extended epiphany to pin down extempore thinking
like a butterfly pinned on a board a hoard a treasure
trove of words spread out like wings aflutter in the
eternal breeze the sneeze of time the wind of
consciousness filling the sail the spinnaker ballooning
and there is no plot as there is none in life there is only
the stutter of wording between waking and sleeping,
the little cicada of consciousness singing with its legs
in Provence summer heat the bleat of sheep under the
hill the mistral wind in the lavender carrying the scent
of the race oh what a spurious fabrication so let's
return to the real world down to earth in a tram in the

South Bronx and somebody reading the daily blatt on
the way to perform in the Yiddish theatre Lower East
Side or are we riding the Staten Island Ferry during
the Second World War or landing in San Francisco on a
ferry from Oakland oh all the same tick of time in a
clock tower and eternal spring coming ever returning
but for how much longer Aye mates tell me that in the
morning blatt will I find our fate written there or in
any ledger or Bible tell me that Tell me tell me the
moon in the Hebrides and the fog falling down like a
scrim in London and sister in the street her brassiere
backward ain't that a pretty picture of this life on earth
and all tears are the same and yet we go on living
because we love it love it love it yes and some of this
country founded by slave owners who wanted to be free
oh yeah it's the American dream but you have to be
asleep to believe it and so what else is new and where
do we go from here Are we back at Square One with
the newborn babe carrying with him all the genes of
the race and what a race it is A foot race a camel race a
horse derby with all the bets on unknown ponies on an
Ellis Island merry-go-round with all the riders reaching
out for the brass ring and where do we get on or off Ah
none of that I am merely speaking my mind such as it
is and that's all there is to it this long blab on
Blabbermouth Night the endless night filled with the
rabble babble of a billion tongues all wagging at once
in falsetto, boisterous polyphoboisterous panhandlers

all drunk on street corners Brother can you spare a
dame or how about carrying me for a block and have
you seen the Rose of Tralee who is pining away for me
somewhere over the sea Blarney be Oh it's just my
seabag full of memories and I am a tear of the sun I
am a hill where poets run I invented the alphabet after
watching the flight of cranes who made letters with
their legs I am a word in a tree I am a hall of poetry I
am a raid on the inarticulate I have dreamt that all my
teeth fell out but my tongue lived to tell the tale I am a
hill of poetry I am a bank of song I am a player piano
in an abandoned casino on a seaside esplanade in a
dense fog still playing, I am an American I was an
American boy I read the *American Boy* magazine and
became a Boy Scout in the suburbs I thought I was
Tom Sawyer catching crayfish in the Bronx River and
imagining the Mississippi, I had a baseball mitt and an
American Flyer bike, I delivered the *Woman's Home
Companion* at five in the afternoon and the *Herald
Trib* at five in the morning, I still can hear the paper
thump on lost porches, I saw Lindbergh land, I looked
homeward and saw no angel, I got caught stealing
pencils in the five-and-ten-cent store the same month I
made Eagle Scout, I chopped trees for the CCC and sat
on them, I landed in Normandy in a rowboat that
turned over, I have seen the educated armies on the
beach at Dover, I have seen the garbagemen parade in
the Columbus Day Parade behind the fat farting

trumpeters, I have eaten potato salad and dandelions at
anarchist picnics, I have eaten hot dogs in ballparks, I
have ridden boxcars boxcars boxcars, I have traveled
among unknown men, I was with Noah in the Ark, I
was in India when Rome was built, I was in the manger
with an ass, I have seen the Laughing Woman in Luna
Park outside the Fun House in a great rainstorm still
laughing, I have heard the sound of revelry by night, I
have wandered lonely as a crowd, I have engaged in
silent exile and cunning, I flew too near the sun and
my wax wings fell off, I am looking for my Old Man
whom I never knew, I am looking for the Lost Leader
with whom I flew. Young men should be explorers.
Home is where one starts from. Womb-weary I rest I
have traveled, I have seen goof city, I have heard Kid
Ory cry, I have heard a trombone preach, I have heard
Debussy strained thru a sheet, I have slept on a
hundred islands where books were trees, I have heard
the birds that sound like bells I have worn grey flannel
trousers and sold what sells I have dwelt in a hundred
cities where trees were books. What subways What
taxis What cafés! What women with blind breasts limbs
lost among skyscrapers, I have seen the statues of
heroes at carrefours, Danton weeping at a Metro
entrance, Columbus in Barcelona pointing westward
up the Ramblas toward the American Express, Lincoln
in his stony chair and a great Stone Face in North
Dakota. I read the want ads daily looking for a stone a

leaf an unfound door. I hear America singing in the
Yellow Pages. One could never tell the soul has its
rages. It is long since I was a herdsman, oh I went to
the city and I did weep, out of touch with nature in a
megalopolis maybe with the human crowd about to
wander off a cliff somewhere yes that same bunch that
grew up from apes after dinosaurs became birds and
elephants grew trunks by the banks of the great
grey-green greasy Limpopo River long ago in a
universe that is not conscious but is rather a blind
creature a blind creation by a blind creator motivated
by a blind life force unconscious of itself the goddess
Ka in Egyptian mythology and all we can do is adopt a
Stoic philosophy as Buddhists do to recognize our
blind fate and yet to enjoy the journey and even laugh
aloud as Zen fools do in their craaazy wisdom to think
of the absolute absurdity of it all after all for are we
not all clowns doing our cartwheels around the earth
and the sun setting in all its burning glory And the life
of the mind connecting to the struggle for justice is a
way of life but what did I know about all that when I
was growing up in that small suburb when all I knew
to begin with was the barbaric heart in the geography
of nowhere before I discovered the fruit on the tree of
sex but what do you mean sex is ruining everything
You must be a kook or something Well so let me tell
you I mean that the single root problem in the whole
world the problem of problems underlying all the ills of

the world can be traced back to overpopulation like
why is there so much pollution because there are too
many cars and too many coal-burning plants because
too many people want cars and heat etc etc and why
are they cutting down the rain forests because they
need the wood to build more houses for more and more
people and so on and on all because people won't stop
making love or just fucking They just won't stop it or
even cut down on their amorous or orgiastic activity
like Man you can't tell me how many lovers I can have
or how many babies I make you fascist you're taking
away my basic freedoms my basic human rights and
ain't this a free country so go fuck yerself komrad and
on and on so that the earth is overflowing with two-
legged creatures and nothing to do about it because to
propagate is a basic undeniable instinct yes we have a
blind instinctual primeval urge to propagate and
reproduce ourselves and we're going to do it no matter
what and we're never never going to stop fucking and
so cover her head with an American flag and fuck for
Old Glory oh it's a long night that ends in day and it's
the short happy life of Francis Macomber and the long
unhappy life of John Doe-re-me-me-me oh where to
begin and where to end Mother mine what have we
here a bit of protoplasm grown into a boy or man or
woman and what is it this strange creation never before
seen in eternity Love's Labor's Lost and all that Tell
me tell me a tale of me-me-me or he-he-he the sound of

laughter interspersed with tears and if I weren't
laughing I'd be crying or vice versa or twice worser So
that so that life is a short day's journey and Blimey if it
ain't dark in here I can't see beyond my nose if that far
if at all and that's the long and the short of it after all
as my monkey mind raves on But did I not lift my lamp
or did she lift her lamp beside the golden door Ah yes
but now who's closing the door and scratching out the
stone inscription so that it reads Don't send me your
poor your whatever yearning to be free Don't give me
that I've had enuf of all that and I have my own pursuit
of happiness to pursue and don't disturb me in that
happy pursuit and there are other kinds of doors
smaller and smaller doors or lead doors instead of gold
doors and the hinges may get changed anyway to swing
both ways or not at all and the whole idea of doors is
hilarious as when I engaged in a long discussion on the
phone with poet Philip Lamantia when he was
expositing on L'Âge d'Or and I was raving about
starting a literary magazine called *Large Door* and the
two of us went on and on enthusing about our two
subjects and both thinking we were talking about the
same thing on and on until we were disconnected and
in fact he died Gone gone into the great dark brother
Let there be light while the rest of us go on living on
the spinning earth and the truth will out as long as
there is light the light of night and the light of day so
let's just say that if we live forever in the light the truth

will out and justice will reign or rain down on us like
manna or bananas from heaven as if such a high place
ever existed and L'Âge d'Or will return again when we
will all be beautiful creatures naked in sun and happy
as the day is long loving each other without envy or
hate all open-armed and openhearted to each other
without fear and trembling or paranoia all the while
striving to piece together the past and the future to
make some sense of it and in the end to try to fathom
man's fate the aim of all art painted or written in
hieroglyphs or computer code with ciphers for eternity
and infinity the Pi of our lives on earth or elsewhere
for what else have we to do on earth but figure out how
and why we're here and will we all ever meet again in
darkness or in light the moon is rising and shadows
bound about the landscape like svelte ghosts smoking
hookahs in our dreams and all is mystery and we are
all mysterious even to each other stick figures on the
far horizon dancing on the edge of the world signaling
to us Hello! Hello! are we not all brothers man and
dame are we not all one and I am you passing thru the
ultimate Golden Door to fall through space forever
organic tossed upon the solar wind our winding sheet
forever unwinding Let us pray or prey upon each other
like wild beasts or wilderbeasts upon a plain where
humanoids first emerged from apes in the heart of
darkest Africa the nameless night shattered with light
and my real brother heard my first cry in a small back

bedroom in Yonkers New York and I sprang up and ran
off into the jungles of the world through thickets of
feeling dense woods of emotion forests of fast friends
and enemies swamps of paranoia sloughs of despond
high hills of happiness breakthroughs of mind and
imaginary adventures of the imaginary soul

 WITH the mind still raving away on its own and
poetry not an expression of emotion but an escape
from it said old Tea Ass Eliot he of Saint Louey posing
as a perfect British gentleman with his tragic wife
Vivienne with her menstrocity and poor Tom letting
it all out finally in his *Four Quartets* with all his pain
well hidden in its lovely prose poetry the year before
she died in a private asylum but nevermind all that
and let's just dance instead and "Have a nice day"
says the rear-guard painter while buttering his toast
with dollars but you can't have a nice day when it's
night and we spend half our lives in darkness and
so bless Mr. Edison for bringing us out of the great
dark yes the great dark comes upon us every twelve
hours and we must all sleep through at least half of
it every night or we'll all croak yes we are required
to sleep and to dream yes we absolutely must dream
and we are such stuff as dreams are made into We are
the great dreamers although maybe not so great as
other animals like dogs and cats and other animals
that hibernate whole winters Can you imagine what
they could all be dreaming and dreaming all that

time and isn't it strange how every night when we lie
down our brains are put into a coma and our muscles
are incapacitated and we cannot move or run when a
monster or phantom appears on our dream-screen and
we cannot swim when in our dreams we are thrown
from a sinking ship into the sea and all we can do is lie
there with mouths agape awaiting the next apocalypse
or revelation and it better be Sweet Dreams or else
we end up moaning or weeping so where does it all
leave us back here on earth on a pillow with weak
echoes or flashbacks of scenes we have just dreamed
yes flashbacks of some lost existence in some forgotten
world or landscape over the horizon never seen when
waking so here we are just you and just me sitting on
our zafu cushions or at bars in happy hours or working
or playing or fucking or laughing or crying and sighing
or otherwise living it up in our casino Land of the
Brave and Holy Smokes ain't it cool to be alive ain't it
awesome yeah and I am American or a space traveler
just touched down here for a few millennia before
taking off for new virgin undespoiled planets or pieces
of stardust for are we not all pure stardust adrift in
endless space in a dream within a dream in which
texts in our consciousness are jumbled together with
the Bible and cut-ups from *Naked Lunch* or want ads
mixed with highway signs in North Dakota advertising
Unisex Hair Saloons etc etc And "It's been a long
day already, I've been up all night" said the Ohlone

Indian occupying Alcatraz on Thanksgiving and the
Feds moved in and you know the drill but the braves
come back anyway every Thanksgiving beating their
drums against the Pilgrims in riot gear who in New
England in an incredible act of mercy had decided
to eat turkey instead of Indians indeed indeed but
wasn't Mr. Edison's little light really no more than an
artificial spark whereas it was really Gautama Buddha
who showed us the true way out of the great dark so
that if we chant the Great Paramita Sutra or Mantra
of Compassion we just might attain enlightenment yes
if we chant the six syllables of Om Mani Padme Hum
then our Pride Jealousy Desire Ignorance Greed and
Anger might be transformed into pure light even in
the midst of our avaricious industrial uncivilization
with its brilliant selling of samsara and its barren
distractions oh yes our great consumer society a
fanatical religion with its omnivorous consumer
machine devouring us and its vampire electronics
sucking our lifeblood while I am just a Zen fop
with the Humbug wandered abroad and all this my
boozy wisdom but my idol all the time is Siddhartha
under the Bodhi Tree seeking enlightenment but
then again there are all sorts of other ways to try to
seek enlightenment and peeling a potato to find the
real potato could possibly be enlightening or you
could just maybe pay some taxi driver to let you get
in the trunk of his cab while he drives around for a

certain amount of time all the while trusting he won't
forget about you and leave you in there until you get
enlightened by dying when you will no doubt see some
eternal light and hear the voice of the fourth person
singular directing you which way to walk And it's Om
Om Om all the way into eternity Oh so I am just an
onion peeling myself down to the core to find there is
nothing there at all and thus attaining the same end
as the most advanced guru and ain't that funny but is
it funny-ha-ha or funny-pathetic that's what I want to
know yes like they say life is a comedy to those who
think and a tragedy to those who feel or is it the other
way around take your choice and roll your dice oh it's
nice to think of yourself as having free will but all
water is not tears and who knows if the cries of birds
are cries of ecstasy or cries of despair and all is not
lost when the sun goes down when red sky at night
is the sailor's delight and the dark side of the moon
holds many mysteries which light will never reveal yes
the moon after much reflection says "Sun is God" and
standing still the river rushes forward (carrying a leaf
upon which we are stranded passengers)

  AND so then into the void in our Ark or Crystal
Palace whose foundations founder in water yes the
great construct of our electronic civilization built of
crystal chips invulnerable except to the slightest drop
of water striking it dead in the coming floods And the
kid in the basement not the underground man but

the underwater man babbling incoherent imbecilities
ha-ha don't you believe it for he wasn't born a mindless
rebel and didn't become one by joining some bomb-
throwing idiots in some sweet act of violence no sir it
was no doubt all because of a lack of love at a tender
age yes sir let me tell you it had nothing to do with a
fanatical urge to fight injustice everywhere and change
the world oh no none of that it was rather that this
kid started out deprived of a mother or father and had
no family of his own and if he had had a real one he
wouldn't have turned out the way he is today no sir a
life among strangers at an early age is a life without
love and the kid grows up unfeeling yes that's it the kid
who never got an embrace or a kiss until he grew up
and met a warm woman his age this little kid's youth
was a trauma of loneliness and unfeeling yes he was
a stranger among strangers and a stranger to himself
full of longing for he knew not For what could he know
since there was no one to tell him anything and he
could not even know that what he was longing for was
love Oh how would he know that who knew only kind
strangers or not-so-kind strangers and so whom does
he turn to when he grows up and shakes his trauma
or tries to find some feeling with others and to whom
does he naturally fall in with if not with other lost
souls or alienated bodies and thereby hangs the tale
of alienation from all the Others the regular people
of normal life and normal society yes the tale of the

haves and have-nots those who had love or had it not
And so life groped on in darkness and light oh it's an
old story isn't it and you can read about it in endless
novels and endless poems of alienation and despair
and who the hell wants to hear about it again except if
the poor author can come up with some new exciting
twist worthy of a production on reality TV and people
who have real families are incapable of understanding
the loneliness on earth felt by orphans from birth
especially at holiday times when families gather as he
remembered one snowy Christmas in that suburban
village where there was a hotel on a hill all covered
with snow and there was a Christmas pageant scene
going on with a baby in a manger and the Wise Men
approaching the manger bearing gifts from Saks Fifth
Avenue and Mary in the manger and all that while the
snow is falling on everything on the village main street
where he was standing looking up and the air oozing
with Christmas carols like "Joy to the World the Lord
has come" and everyone hurrying by with presents or
packages of things for home and "Joy to the World"
ringing out and maybe kids going by on sleds pulled by
their fathers etc etc you get the scene like you've seen
it a million times reenacted over and over the Babe
in the manger because they claim there was no room
in the inn yeah yeah Oh happy day with this little kid
standing there on the frozen corner Oh man Look
homeward angel now and melt with wrath

AS "In sorrow I gaze upon my generation" wrote
Lermontov in a poem a couple of hundred years
ago way off over there in Russia while here and now
someone has discovered a new alkaloid in the brain
called idiotine presumably the ingredient that makes
idiots and there's a lot of it to go around oh these
are wintry thoughts and there are terrible nights of
lightning and thunder and rain as if the sun or moon
would never come back again as one night when I
could not feel my heartbeat and could not find my
pulse on my wrist but found it in my watch on my
other wrist tick-tick the tolling of eternity oh what
unending nights but summer comes and life changes
and I still can enjoy a laugh that sounds like an
accordion yes after all there still are things that make
life worth living or wasting yes plenty of them in fact
yes oh white nights and mouths of desire and what of
the hidden call of the morning dove mourning his love
what of the sun streaming down in meshes of morning
high tide and the heron's call and figures on the beach
running into the sea laughing heads thrown back long
hair streaming forever young ah life goes on with the
cries of boat-tailed grackles in the tops of jacaranda
trees in the setting sun at San Miguel de Allende but
still in sorrow I gaze upon our twenty-first-century
civilization with its casino culture its electronic pulse
its stone heart its brain dumbed-down and let the bad
times roll But now a dead silence rings in my ears and

life seems to have come to a standstill and I don't know
which way to go from here as if there were only one
way to go as if all were ordained ahead of time the first
step of the baby out of the crib determining his whole
itinerary but what am I to do just sit here dribbling
words on a page as if that were the most important
thing in life as if it could amount to anything or give
anyone an inspiration on how to live or die or whatever
indeed let us spray said one skunk to another in the
church So here we go and keep going on and on with
our crazy thoughts round and round in the squirrel's
cage in the mandala maze in the endless spinning of
the skein of living and the river rushes forward with us
on it as on a tossing raft floating down the great flood
with Jim and Huck into the heartland oh brother can
you spare your cornball comments on my way of life
and where I came from and where I'm going and what's
it to anybody if I'm an Okie who fled the dust bowl to
Californiay in the 1930s or a sexy French-Swiss hosiery
salesman pushing silk stockings on Barbary Coast
ladies of the night Man oh man if I could enumerate
all the men and women and dogs and cats of the world
and describe each of them in great detail with all their
tails and tics and passions Well then would I have given
you even the slightest inkling of what makes life tick
what makes the world clock go round It's a hopeless
task and even Shakespeare or Chekhov couldn't begin
to articulate what Sophocles heard by the Aegean long

ago or what Shiva heard dancing on many legs in the
dawn of time and if one man cries out then another
hears it and he cries out and his woman cries out and
their dog picks it up and starts howling and when one
dog barks the whole pack picks it up and starts howling
their muzzles to the sky but all it takes is for one big
hyena to start laughing and then the whole world rocks
with laughter the laughter of the mock Absurd the
whole world a Theatre of the Absurd—oh so that's your
way out of the big dilemma You think that's some kind
of solution man that's just another evasion don't give
me that Absurd bullshit and don't give me all those
other Absurd answers to fathom our fate on earth even
as the curtain comes down on the last act Wow did I
say our last act and *après nous le déluge?* and there's
an ex–Lutheran minister telling me "We ain't coming
back We believe in resurrection not in reincarnation
like the Buddhists" which explains why he was
stretched out on a lounge chair in the lobby outside of
where his Jewish-Buddhist girlfriend was meditating
with her Tibetan guru and "Yeah" he sed "she's a
Ju-Bu" and so then when they were all thru meditating
for the day I'm introduced to the big chief guru who
says "You from around here?" like I was from Squaw
Valley or Tahoe where the retreat was happening and
I says "Yes I'm from the universe" thinking I was
being real clever and real mystic at the same time
only he just gives me a funny look thinking Who is

this creep? and shakes my hand hard and smiles his
love at me, saying "I'll see ya again" "Yes yes" I say as
he turns away and I'm thinking Does he mean he'll
see me on earth or someplace else and so off we went
on our own separate paths around the universe and
that's the-he-and-the-she of it bye-bye blackbird and
may the good Lord save us if He really exists with
all the odds against Him yeah yeah put that in your
sebsi and smoke it and thus deprive yourselves of the
comfort of great religions dreamed up by the wisest
men and women thru thousands of years and giving
you something to live by yes some gods to live by for
every great people needs them and what great myths
do we have today to live by (go read Joseph Campbell
and weep) and who are our idols except football or
baseball or rock stars or military heroes yeah tell me
tell me why not instead wake up each morning with a
great Hooray! leading of course to a Last Hurrah! and
each day a new invention a new form of living just like
picking up a new pen every morning and reinventing
an alphabet and inventing a new genre neither a
novel nor a memoir nor a form of documentary but
an unnamable piece of day and night spoken or sung
by the voice of the fourth person singular and what is
that voice if it is not the very voice that is doing the
thinking when we meditate yes just ask yourself who is
thinking when you are meditating or just ruminating
half awake at four in the morning when that dark dove

with flickering tongue passes below the horizon of
our living—or fully awake at midday yes whose is that
voice whispering to your mind when you are silent and
alone Oh is it not the voice of consciousness itself and
consciousness itself a single ludic voice inside each of
us the voice for magical thinking

   AS if I had such a voice or verse sitting in some
café where you'd think nothing never happens but
let me tell you plenty goes down in the back rooms
of the mind and heart at the back tables while some
hairy dude is playing a mandolin with its sweet sad
sound the very soul of old Italy as at the beginning
of *Godfather II* but then this dame comes prancing
up to me and Oh, she sez, I'm only trying to keep in
shape, and I say Right on but when do I get to see your
shape Yeah yeah, she says, so come up and see me
some other time, but somehow it never happens, one
of those dopey dreams if you know what I mean And
so is sex still driving everything or isn't it Oh samsara
is good for you and to deprive us of all the pleasures
of our sensorium may be to die Oh I was zaptized by
the fish-eaters when I was a helpless babe but somehow
escaped thank you very much so don't attempt to dip
me again in that holy puddle man oh man the direct
or alternating current of my consciousness does not
desire to be short-circuited with any kind of liquid
except the ilk of human kindness a different kind
of liquid whose genetic code has still to be cracked

and how lonely is Christ these days like this noon as
I was passing the church of Saint Peter and Paul and
the big sad synthetic bell was tolling twelve strokes
very slow and no one inside at all not a soul in sight
not even a priest *oy vey* . . . while in spring the earth
sings as if it knew love songs by heart while a sense of
loss still pervades poetry past and present oh what is
it in us that prefers singing of loss instead of present
ecstasies and why are we always trying to stamp out
the burning fires of samsara whereas we could just be
lying back to hear the primordial sound of the universe
the subdued murmur of the sea-tide setting inward as
Rinpoche wrote while living and dying while chanting
the great mantra om mani padme hum that transforms
pride jealousy desire ignorance greed and anger into
something nude and strange while our consumer
machine goes on brilliantly selling "samsara and its
barren distractions" yeah oh modern industrial society
is a fanatical religion all the while killing everywhere
the natural bardo of life so do I instead go not with the
Poets of Loss but with the great yea-sayers the great
yes-sayers like Whitman and Henry Miller yes why lie
down with the dead ahead of time Life can turn on
a dime and the next thing you know you're king or
married to a Queen of Hearts or playing darts with
death on some foreign battlefield like Ulysses or lost in
a labyrinth of your own making with only a Minotaur
for a friend And so and so be sure to meditate with

your eyes open yes your eyes the jewels of your
head while I unlock my word-hoard of ruminations
meditations exhortations celebrations condemnations
excitations lamentations liberations and ecstasies
plotless as a life that is to say like a life whose plot is
only discovered after it is lived oh blimey ain't that a
mouthful but speaking of yea-sayers there's a species
of ape who never make war and spend all their time
making love with whoever comes to hand and there are
no social prohibitions restricting their lovemaking with
whoever suits their fancy and they never make war
with foreign tribes but peacefully join them and make
love with them too so that they are always sexually
satisfied and are drained of all primordial bestial
bloodlust or imperatives to kill even as human hunters
came after them for their meat in the deep African
forests which are now being cut down and thus pass
the glories of the world the bestial kingdom destroyed
And what are you going to do about it my dear friend
just what's to be done is the whole world population
a dysfunctional family on a boat heading for the falls
and how steep the drop into oblivion and what does
American Legion Post 101 have to say about it You're
on Nickelodeon TV so say something intelligent tell
us who we are and where we're going and if you're an
artist well then say something important in your art
Man oh man speak up and tell us something true and
how are we to proceed to find the lost city and stop

mumbling and enlighten us and just don't sit there
rocking on your wooden horse Daddy Daddy I am
looking for my father whom I never knew I am looking
for the Lost Leader with whom I flew but perhaps we
should suffer a real cultural revolution and transform
our society into that of the apes who make love all
the time with anyone and everyone yes what if we just
abolished all the prohibitions and inhibitions in our
religious and moral codes and just let loose all our
suppressed desires and hungers oh what then with
our sexual lava flowing freely and no longer seething
under the surface of polite society yes what then if not
paradiso? yes yes except except what of the resulting
surge of population on an earth already groaning
with overpopulation to the extent that all of our most
fatal world problems are directly traceable back to it?
Enough! Enough! Lower your penis, you rapacious
dog, down, Rover, down! Sing hallelujah and life goes
on and it's *poids net* nowhere and the jury is still out
at the World Court trying the case of the Lord and
is He/She guilty of crimes against humanity? what
an obscene question what a blasphemous idea to be
bringing God to judgment as if He/She or It could
be tried and found guilty or innocent but in fact the
case before the court is still in the discovery stage
trying to uncover the facts so that both the prosecutor
representing the Establishment and the Defender of
the People will know all the facts of the case which so

far has proved impossible since all have bathed in the
River of Forgetfulness and the River of Hypnos yet still
the future is always with us as is the present and the
past but when the future becomes the present does it
lose its lustre if not its mystery yet we still recapture
that lustre by involuntary memory or would you just
call it nostalgia the past revisited as if by a ghost of
ourselves and my mind a labyrinth trying to find the
way out speaking with all the voices of *l'homme moyen
sensuel* telling all his stories sounding all his cries
and laughter and Everyman's mind and tongue are
mine my consciousness my unbound tongue let loose
wandering through all our lives thinking together in
the night of magical thinking to find the Sibyl with
arms upraised and holding up that Golden Bough
in a painting by Turner as the sun rises hidden in
mists of morning with our collective consciousness a
butterfly flittering over the landscape of living and all
that sexual lava seething beneath the surface of polite
society

    AND a coracle upon the sea a fisherman in it
drawing his nets and a high voice calling as dusk falls
and the light drops suddenly into night oh is that then
all there is to life a little light and then night again
over and over Oh I had my hour my one fat fierce
sweet hour There was a shout about my ears There
was something in the air that night the stars were
bright but then the day came which made absolutely

no sense at all but if you don't stir up your mind all the
time it will become clear like a pool of water, said the
Buddha, even as the past recedes at an ever-increasing
pace and civilization as we know it going down the
drain faster and faster as "Man with his burning soul
has but an hour of breath to build a ship of Truth in
which his soul may sail—sail on the sea of death for
death takes toll of beauty, courage, youth, of all but
Truth" and it's three strikes and you're out at the
Old Ball Game as a red ant walks with its many legs
along an ochre wall above the sea its round eye seeing
everything including Odysseus passing by in the Strait
of Messina at Scylla far off a voice is calling in the
dawn wind and the swart ship with rowers at the locks
the pilot casting his plumb line sounding the depths
of the straits with its rocky shoals its treacherous
shallows its rude winds gusting and Odysseus the chief
pirate hovering over the helmsman the battered hull
thumping against the running sea but Odysseus steers
apart he knows the sound he knows the apparition
when in a dense fog strange alluring shapes loom of
a sudden before him and it's La Lupa the Wolf the
fog that eats ships and men far from home far from
home with Scylla and Charybdis to sail through and
the sirens calling And it's the portrait of the artist
as an old man and it's still the same old story of the
young buck who leaves his home and his mother and
father and brothers and sisters to find his own solitary

way in a world of his own imagining which is not
necessarily the real world as it exists and so off into
the wild blue yonder to find oneself with pants down
at the Folies Bergère or by the door of a church whose
name he'd rather not remember Ah yes and my mind
my constant companion through the archipelagos and
uplands of thinking where I love to roam and stumble
or swim with or against any current as wild winds
blow our arks made of thoughts Blimey me if it ain't
the usual illusions when in dead of night we hear the
far sounds that only night can produce hark hark the
field mice stir and birds in the bush converse before
dawn as we turn and turn in bed our eyes still fed with
darkness and it is the time of final reckoning of the
never-ending end of night the time to get real after a
lifetime of illusion and evasion yes now is the hour to
let it all loose and let it come down to the real to the
way life really is the bones of reality of the here and
now I hear the muezzin calling from his tower Brother
observe the time and repent! brother brother and
where now in the dense fog that drifts along pavements
and wraps around lampposts and tin figures lost in
it fleeing and Big Ben sounds through it all as if all
empires had not already crumbled Night night and
where is my lover mother sister mister and who shall
show us the way show me the way oh brother oh sister
let's go down down to the river to pray if not to prey
upon each other the end is just beginning and we'll

to the woods no more to snore upon others' dreams
and hear the ladies gossiping about who slept with
whom and what the parrot said and thereafter never
spoke again and ain't it a sin the way men and women
carry on thru the centuries on and on demoiselles and
handymen hunkered down in their hovels or palazzos
peasants all! whites bleached out from blacks out of
Africa in the beginning before it all began oh shall we
cruise awhile with Odysseus through the strait once
more or cast ashore in some sunny isle for good and
forever and hark hark the lark at heaven's gate sings?
Oh is that any way to come at the Real and my mind
still stuck in its own mire of desire and giving my
body its misdirections nude erections rude exorcisms
ejaculations epiphanies and revelations and aperçus
all masturbations of the mind and the boat never
beaches in the reaches of night night But I must arise
and go now to the Isle of Manisfree where there are
no beds with memory-mattresses that remember and
record everyone who ever slept there and with whom
or without whom they slept man or woman or a third
sex of which there are many yes but do I have to go
via the Rome airport Fiumicino named after some
crooked river and thousands of joyless travelers laden
with huge bags all on the life journeys or already
passed through Dante's gates that tell you to "Abandon
hope all ye who enter here" and you're now in one of
The Divine Comedy's crude nude circles descending

toward Hell or ascending to Paradiso the light at the
end of the tunnel *mamma mia* well it's evident that
I am not capable of seeing the world for Real since I
keep drifting off into these fantasies or pipe dreams or
other evasions etc etc and where's the reality of it all
ha-ha well if you think for one moment that I'm going
to reveal to you any unvarnished unadorned naked
truth If you think you're going to learn from me any
secrets of the universe or of the human heart well then
you're a bigger idiot than I supposed so you might as
well stop reading this drivel in the middle of the night
so bye-bye baby just leave me to my mutterings because
I can't go on but I go on with the bleached-out memoirs
torn poems fished out of wastebaskets full of ordinary
platitudes and all the brilliant things I was going to say
at lunch mixed with secrets of the universe gone down
the drain or misplaced in psychedelic hallucinations
but what's below the drain may turn out to be the most
interesting to keep you awake in the general slaughter
of life as she is lived today when it is dawn and the
world goes forth to murder dreams And is not life in
general a great battle eternal between optimism and
pessimism between yea-sayers and nay-sayers between
the naïve and the cynical between joy and joy-killers
between lovers and weepers between joie de vivre and
nausea in the Sartrean sense or between light and
dark between blinding light and deep darkness and
all existence a struggle between the bearable lightness

of Good and dark dark Evil even here in Paris in
the spring with pure light filtering through the
marronniers and the sunlight flooding my mind with
the lyricism that kills all laments even as a huge black
crow flies across my path in the park of Saint-Julien-
le-Pauvre And close by I hear twelve slow strokes of an
iron bell

AND a young stud at the next table typing on his
laptop, both ears stopped with earphones. A flock of
birds wheels by in the sky. One of them falls to the
pavement right in front of us. A black car, a farting
bus, a bicycle go by. So does a blond with a baby and a
dog barking furiously. I'm just five feet from the guy.
Finally I say in a friendly voice, "You from around
here? Haven't seen you before in the neighborhood."
No answer. He continues typing, staring at the laptop.
He heard nothing? Is this body alive? I'm alarmed.
I call 911. After some time a cop car arrives and he's
arrested for "nonparticipation in humanity." They haul
the corpse away.

SO then "dancing on the edge of the world"
sang some Indian on the far shore of San Francisco
before it became a Pale Face city and Indians danced
on Alcatraz before Pale Face made Alcatraz into a
prison to jail all the outcasts and halfcasts on a stolen
continent where Pale Face taught us to drink hot
brown water in the morning and cold brown water
at night firewater in bottles on street corners on

lost reservations in indigenous chaos And ain't that
the long and the short of it the life and death of the
Indian Nation while the rest of us were spooning
along hot on the trail of instant gratification or not
so instant maybe but get your own and devil take the
rear quarters of the beast of life but the old Indian
myth of San Francisco once being an island still
persisted among the Pale Face who took over several
centuries ago and the myth persisted as late as the
middle of the twentieth century when still on the
streets of San Francisco you could encounter citizens
who thought of San Francisco as a kind of offshore
republic not really a part of the greater United States
yes indeed San Franciscans then still had a kind of
insular island mentality and all descended from the
first nonbourgeois settlers of San Francisco wildcat
gold seekers layabouts gamblers whores drifters con
men card sharks and rogue cowboys from the open
range before the West was fenced and Civil War draft
evaders and ladies of easy virtue as they was called
yeah man the first settlers of San Francisco a veritable
rogues gallery with sailors and seafarers from all over
the world and robber barons and well you name it It
was a fine scurvy crew ready for anything including
the earthquake and fire of 1906 yeah yeah and that
the beginning for a whole new ball game a whole new
city rising from the ashes "like a phoenix" they said
and it was true that is if you had hit gold or a rich

widow or a jackpot somewhere And our hero almost *al
verde* as they say in *italiano* walking up Market Street
after crossing Oakland ferry like Whitman Crossing
Brooklyn Ferry or so he thought with his seabag still
with him slung over his shoulder but no albatross still
in it since he had shuffled it off in Paris and so into
the new world and the last frontier as if it still existed
in the Wild West of our imagination where the Actor's
Workshop in San Francisco later performed *Waiting
for Godot* before the waiting inmates in San Quentin
Prison those specialists in waiting who do nothing
but wait for some unimaginable liberator and so left
it up to us the inmates of the world all of us spinning
through space on the surface of this turning place
from which we cannot escape at least not most of us
except for those privileged to catch a seat in some
future spacecraft heading for some other star ha-ha
as if they could actually live on it once they got there
disembarked into the ultimate unimaginable oh man
Do you dig? the days spin past and we are but birds
upon some divine vine the grapes of some ecstatic vino
we hope to drink and why not just press the grapes of
wrath rather than all the other varietals of grapes and
other psychedelics oh peel me a grape Cleopatra and
turn me on yes the days are endless on this drifting
barge on the Nile of our dreams oh what an illusion
but what's wrong with illusions for if you take away
a man's illusions he will die as in some play like *The*

Iceman Cometh or *The Time of Your Life* waiting
in a bar for illusions to materialize or in San Quentin
or in other places where everybody's waiting for
something or someone and so make up your own
illusion by looking at yourself in any mirror on the
wall of your dreams or in any still pool where fireflies
wink And our hero having read Saroyan's *My Name
Is Aram* when he was fifteen 1930s with crazy Indian
chiefs riding around in limousines "feet up and
smoking wild cigars" or like Jack London's Frisco long
ago when "Don't Call It Frisco" became the cry of the
nabobs living on Nob Hill who didn't like drunken
riffraff sailors down on the waterfront singing "Frisco"
    AND the mind winging away on its own even
before it sees the light of day or even after its body
can no longer function tick-tick the brain mumbles
on or sings on according to its predilections tragic or
lyric comic or *curioso* on and on into the night and
every thought I think is my last thought and my first
thought just born into the sentient world oh if I could
find and think my first thought again what a revelation
what a sense-ation what a watta in first light upon
earth O Paradiso or disheveled landscape Dante be
damned we're out in the dear daylight winging away
and our life on earth a rave a raving in pure light
shining in all things and creations and so on and
so forth or dreaming away like gents old and full of
sleep yeah yeah that's another way to go when I have

nothing more to say but keep on saying it over and
over Shall I say it again Well then say something new
for a change instead of same old tired mythologies of
the past as time with its feather still strolls lines in
everybody's faces while sometimes in darkness and
thunder miracles light up the land like the beauty of
human figures male and female in all those cheesecake
magazines at checkout counters all across America
yes those checkout counters the very concrete gates of
reality through which we all have passed into the very
panorama of America where every bush burns when
the TV lights are turned up and life still stirs in the
underbrush while everything is recorded by Google in
a Recorded Future in which Peak Empire the peak of
American Empire has been passed and said Empire
has indeed collapsed while its successor the American
Republic (based strictly upon the boundaries of North
America) is flourishing and a happy breed of men in
this little New World is free in our beautiful land in
which the past remains eternally unchangeable and
real while the present is always changeable and surreal
and you should still never play cards with a man called
Doc while the world spins on and it ain't never oveh
until it's oveh . . . And so out here on the late last
frontier, it turns out I am no fucking genius but just
another version of the Middle Mind of America and
so don't expect any great breakthroughs from me as
to the nature of consciousness or any great *aperçus* of

any kind or any Unified Theory of Relative Reality for
our little consciousness is just a candle between two
eternal darknesses yes our little conscious moment is
just a little searchlight trying to pierce the great dark
And I am just waking in the vortex of past time, as if
it were a kind of Nocturama, a structure for animals
that are awake only at night, or this vortex of time
thus becomes a poem with an invisible subject like a
novel that has no plot but wanders around, in which
its characters wander around through life in what
would appear to be an aimless fashion, or at least with
no steady intention or aim, and in the end even the
author has no idea where his back is headed or will
end up, just like life itself, and if art is really supposed
to imitate life we are left with a masterpiece the past
a heap of broken images and the future an infinite
no-man's-land where virgin visions are born out of
pure anarchy while the Buddhists hold that suffering is
the grand end of all being and they devote themselves
to getting through the night of suffering by attaining
enlightenment, that is, the attainment of light, whereas
whereas may not we begin with light as the grand end
of all being and then proceed at last into blue death?
Yes it was the Greeks who said death is blue and I'll
go with that which is much better than considering
death as total darkness made of the Sirocco of Madness
and this my Underground Oratorio But the author
goes right on talking with a kind of insane loquacity

no matter what is happening to the world around him
which is a sure sign of his looniness as can be seen in
mental wards where men sit mumbling to themselves
carrying on serious conversations with themselves
as if everything were sane and rational Oh perhaps
you have seen them as you passed by with firm tread
and it's all like that old film *The King of Hearts* in
which the inmates of an asylum consider themselves
the only sane people in the world while the people
outside go forth every day to murder their dreams
and ecstasies in the general conflagration of everyday
life in the twenty-first century even here on the late
frontier San Francisco which is still an island in the
eyes of the natives indeed indeed when I arrived in
time to witness the end of civilization as we know it in
the final eco-catastrophe and the riven seas come in
to cover us And so is this your AHA moment and am
I the consciousness of a generation or just some old
fool sounding off and trying to escape the dominant
materialist avaricious consciousness of America
today yes escaping into mysticism or enlightenment
or escaping into dope or psychedelics or into pure
lyricism in paint or words yes the lyric escape I am
always indulging in whether in writing or painting or
pure sex as the world turns on driven by testosterone
even in women yes it's still the raised pecker the
joystick that drives the hot car of life O man as I was
pondering our unrelenting destinies as I was thinking

on the good old ways Oh brother let's go down down
to the river to pray Oh yes by god or whoever all you
trans-Americans such as myself Let's go down to the
river to pray Yes trans-Americans indeed for are we
not all from Someplace Else and does it still matter
where we came from and our children not caring
where we came from like passengers on some subway
all from everywhere and all going different places
yet all going where the train is taking them No way
to get off between stops if there are any yes all of us
still in transit so that we must constantly change the
idea of who we are as we go on living in the end-times
the end-times of man on earth while newspapers are
reporting not only that the glaciers are melting and
earth warming but also that the past is receding faster
and faster, like the track behind a speeding-up train
Yes and the train of my life rocking along on these
fictional documentary tracks with no way of telling
what's truly fiction or what's truly documentary (as in
films by Werner Herzog like *Lessons of Darkness* in
which false fantasies and truths are interchangeable)
so that so that who can tell if this tale is a tragicomedy
or a comi-tragedy but in the end I don't go for fatal
endings especially not my own and so and so let's just
say I've summarized my past by theft and allusion
and all I know is that I'll be taking an escalator soon
to the next level of existence or nonexistence and
will it be the down-escalator or the up-escalator and

thereby hangs the tail of this mutt and he still wagging
it And how did he go from a youthful anarchism to
humanitarian socialism as a creed to live by And how
did he end up a painter and a poet always alienated
in one way or another and still claiming that he was
never ingested by the dominant culture that ingests
so many rebels before they croak and he still living in
his own illusion that he's never been ingested as a poet
oh yeah Ah poetry Ain't it all just a lyric escape from
rocky reality but him claiming all the time that poetry
is in fact reality itself the very bedrock essence which
should always be presented without introductions or
prefaces yes just hit them full in the face with the piths
of reality and let there be a sharp intake of air.

AND so the other day I am reading another
handwrit letter from this old girlfriend of mine talking
to me like we never split and so she says: HA! I found
the "old poem" I wrote years ago - it predicted the
present............and funnier than I remembered. I
can't wait for the biography - and the movie. Life is
ironic - if you can keep your sense of humor and lose
your ego (not yours - mine) or rather, and I like this
better, life is absurd - especially how it turns around.
Duchamp, where are you? I should have kept writing
poetry - or become a psychic. If I didn't think you
would collapse laughing I would send you the poem
but I am afraid to. I will wait until you are feeling
better - which will be soon. Remember Kahlil's friend

Dante (love the names) fell off the couch laughing at
Legman's *Rationale of the Dirty Joke* and hurt himself.
I don't want that to happen to you. Keep your chins
up - everything will be fine. It is the waiting that is the
worst. Get out of the hospital as quickly as possible
so you don't get an infraction. Let people take care of
you. Be pampered.......and do not do too much. Don't
push yourself. I am thinking of you - I gave hundreds
of heart milagros to the priests to pray over - if you
believe in that sort of thing - can't hurt and supports
big business (the Catholic Choich). At least you didn't
start your email "........unfortunately for your vacation
plans, etc etc" so the blow was softened. It is amazing
how calluses grow - what would have laid me low a few
years ago is just regular now. I guess that is what life
is also - the inside gets harder and the outside gets
softer (that is an important insight - and a frightening
one). None of this has anything to do with you - this is
all about me so don't take anything personally or get
upset. It's late and I am rambling - and it is not meant
that way, and you told me once to take everything
with a touch of salt and I am not telling you with
a pound of sugar, for I've had so much sugar I am
practically diabetic and I told you I see the world as a
bestiary now - wish that had happened years ago but
if wishes were knishes I'd open a deli - or something
like that. (I'd love a hot pastrami right now - maybe
I am becoming bipolar - see how my mind works - or

doesn't.) I think I am living Edna St. Vincent Millay's life - or else I've just read her too much. You are the only one I know who appreciated her poetry. Everyone else thought she was too sappy. She had a sonnet for everything - and survived. She needed what she needed. I see her as a fox with the heart of a rabbit. I am glad I am a romantic and not a realist - that would be boring and no fun - just the little bit of realism I let in is a drag. I avoid it at all costs. A quote I like is (not from Edna) "never give up and never, under any circumstances, face the facts." That's me...............
and, if I can't talk to you - my oldest dearest longest love, who can I talk to? We didn't talk enough - about important things - us, for instance. I was always too scared (see above). I'll see you again - in my dreams until then. And so how is E. doing? Let me know. He admires you very much - and loves you - but we don't talk about you. We talk about books, ideas, and movies. It is difficult for me to tell - his voice sounds the same. I send him warm clothes and sardines. Chris was here - can't get HIS voice out of my head. The hurricane/storm is frightening - maybe that is what has brought on this mood. I found out who my real father was - took 15 minutes on the computer and cost less than $10..........a little bit of realism almost crept in but I held it at bay. The 1940s census was recently released with all the info - it is a relief of a sort but doesn't really make any difference I am thinking of you.... "If

in the years to come you should remember..." etc... and
today I remembered a trip to Gloucester with you and
that ain't all but just go ahead and fill in the missing
parts and you'll see what you shoulda done with your/
our life, honeybun .....

  AND what am I to do with the rest of my life or
your life as the days rave on, the nights too the long
nights as the daze goes on and where are we anyway
on the face of existence in the race for existence
and which way are we facing with our bullyboy
consciousness But is not laughter the sublime
expression of consciousness which can go from extreme
depression to ecstasy and the final ecstasy nothing
but pure silent laughter Oh the sublimity of it and
if I weren't laughing I'd be dying I'd be crying with
Samuel Beckett and Jimmy Joyce the master laugher
behind the sublime babble of *Finnegan* yeah yeah I
have read it all heard it all heard the falcon in its dying
fall Oh white nights and mouths of desire and the cry
of the mourning dove at dawn and the laughter of the
universe behind closed shutters late at night when
all the world goes sleeping and sleep the suicide of
consciousness and I am entering my silent stage and no
more regurgitation of everything seen or heard or said
over the past century no more of that thank ye and this
no Portrait of the Autist as an Old Man although this
might be my hundredth year to heaven when summer
passed me by and every season became the same

season in my high flat and no one noticed the leaves
coming and going and falling to the cry of flutes and
the dog slept by the TV unaware of spring at the door
leaves in her hair flowered with petals and an ancient
voice in the air singing Primavera! Primavera! And the
wind sprang up at four o'clock that day as it had every
day for a long time a steady wind a great wind sweeping
the universe never ceasing during the late afternoons
and it stirred the leaves of the great laurel tree outside
my window ceaselessly lashing them and it was like
the mistral in southern France except this wind came
from the far far north and still it blows and blows
and blows every day lashing the leaves And the only
sound a high laughter the laughter of the marvelous
the laughter of the invisible the laughter of the absurd
Oh i had not known life had undone so many so many
of my friends on earth all gone and myself shrunk to
an i left with Samuel Beckett the Unnamable almost
underground but still thinking and what does the
spinning spindrift pluriverse care even if it is a kind
of verse for are we all blank verse to the blind cosmos
with its overwhelming indifference to our fate and
our little universe not lyric and good and harmonious
but rather made of total chaos hostility and murder
as Werner Herzog said observing the Grizzly Man
being eaten alive by his favorite grizzly and it's eat or
be eaten all the way down Oh man turn me over i'm
done on this side but nevertheless on the other hand

(and how many hands do we have) perhaps in nature
after all there is a secret innocence hidden beyond the
last savanna deep in some sacred wood wherein I read
the carbon-copy history of creepy man and his far-out
destiny forever shrouded And the real tall-tale story of
your life/my life yet to be told unwinding like a thread
through a labyrinth a labyrêve or an onion peeled
down to its core of Nothingness aha don't you believe
it for there must be more than nothing especially if
you listen to the latest quantum activists telling you
that the cosmos has its own consciousness beyond
the collective consciousness of individuals animal
vegetable or mineral (and this a quantum leap of aha!
insight, sayeth Dr. Goswami) oh man but suppose
on the other hand on the nether hand this cosmos is
nothing but one huge computer in which we are all
micro pixels and everyone knows a computer has no
consciousness of its own but is made up of nothing but
"other" consciousnesses and yet and yet even if all that
is true there might still be a real prophet a bullyboy or
dame a fair-haired one a dark seer or some other form
of conscious talking protoplasm or ecoplasm to light
our way to the final ha-ha! the final aha! the final ah!
which is the final rebellion, and every act of rebellion
expressing a nostalgia for innocence

    OH ain't that going a bit too far with all your misty
mysticism and your ah ah ahs Egad am I supposed
to swallow all that bullshit while I'm trying to drink

my espresso, yeah man as if all this time I was doing
nothing but trying to reach the highest level of
consciousness by emptying my mind of everything Om
Om and the Empty Mind being the end of everything
Nirvana itself so lie back and enjoy ah men and I was
born the same year as Pete Seeger along with Jackie
Robinson Nat King Cole Eva Peron J. D. Salinger Sir
Edmund Hillary who scaled the heights if not the
depths where some so-called heavy thinkers might
have decided that there are Known Knowns and there
are Unknown Knowns and there are also Unknown
Unknowns which are the things we don't know we
don't know since they are beyond our imagination
to imagine And the Unknown Unknowns are where
"god" is or what "god" is "behind the brain" and
"behind the eyes" where all is darkness where all all
is light and does all this mean that I am about to "die"
Well that's a distant possibility although I doubt it
since I of course am an American and Americans don't
die and so I am not about to croak oh no baby not me
not not

SO why does the world, why does the cosmos
exist at all while all the advanced cosmologists have
no answer nor anything but guesses as to which
came first, the Void or the Universe which is like
asking which came first the chick or the egg while
we know all the time it was the cock came first, and
so which came first, Being or Nothingness, and the

existentialists posited that Being (or Existence) came
first, *Essentia* before *Esse,* but no matter which we
are definitely here spinning around on our own little
globe of Earth, and it's Wow! all over again every time
we open our eyes every morning, the sun the sun,
great god sun rising every morn to strike the towers
with a shaft of light even as we sit in cafés endlessly
wasting the time we have to waste time while we
hear manuscripts murmuring like Marcel Proust's
endless sentences simulating endless time in his
"involuntary memory" wherein he found happiness
yes the memory involuntarily thrust upon him by the
sound of a distant bell recalling a bell struck in his
childhood in a moment of happiness or the taste of
that famous madeleine dipped in tea evoking a fleeting
moment with his dear mother yes not the moment
when she refused him the cherished Good-Night Kiss
yes and then there was Tony Judt the intellectual's
intellectual who when he was old and dying and
had lost power of speech he kept thinking back and
back to his childhood and to his Memory Chalet the
place in his early childhood a little inn a *pensione* in
French speaking Switzerland where his family went
on vacation a small cozy inn still there in his old-age
memory where people loved and were loved or felt
fraternity Ah the fate of fraternity in an age of egoism
in which Auguste Comte would brave despair with his
belief that we have an ingrained desire to further the

well-being of others oh what an absurd assumption
And President Obama saying we are all responsible
for each other Ha-ha-ha good luck with your good
intentions in this world where evil really does exist
and functions daily a veritable horned devil with a
pitchfork Evil Evil Evil peeking through the daredevil
fetching smile of a shy instructor or a pleasant lady
with a dog ready to eat you alive And until I was ninety
years old, I never had time to stop and think of where
I was in life while now I look back and see it all too
clearly. I think of Dylan Thomas's "Do not go gentle
into that good night" and of Yeats and the woods of
Arcady being dead, of old the world on dreaming
fed, now Grey Truth her painted toy! Life is still a
freakin' mystery but all that's left now is bare reality
the animals in their field configured grazing on their
reality dreamers all to the end of time

AT the corner of Francisco and Powell the
soundless cars creep by An average Chinese gent
wheels his wobbly bike across the intersection He's
wearing a Mao jacket and leans forward into the steady
north wind as two tourists with tiny backpacks stride
by looking exactly the same dressed the same which is
the man which is the woman There may be only unisex
people left in the world But here are two ladies at the
next table refilling their wineglasses and laughing
and each has a hilarious story to tell they're whooping
it up and one lady says "And what's the opposite of

'booby'?" and the other says "Two boobies!" and they
both haw-haw and almost fall off their chairs here on
the edge of the world and of existence While a girl in
a dirndl skirt lilts by licking an ice-cream cone While
a couple holding hands crosses in front of a delivery
truck which swerves to miss them The two ladies are
still dying laughing as one shouts "Get outa here,
I'm Jewish!" As the Middle Eastern owner of the café
comes by and graces me with a beer While a postman
with empty bag limps across to the PO. The too-hot
sun beats down and the wind continues its flapping
of awnings as four young guys with backpacks stride
by each on his cell phone talking to someone else
somewhere else and instead of Be Here Now it's Be
Somewhere Else Now and I am witnessing Thank God
It's Friday on earth As a Japanese woman in a long
skirt comes out of the Hokkaido studio down the block
As a young husband pushing a stroller sits down at the
café table as the baby bawls and the wife shows up as
the baby continues bawling and the two ladies have
quit laughing and gathered themselves together and
got up saying between laughs "Hope we didn't bother
you! We don't get out much!" And the sun falls down
out of sight on the far horizon

    SO watching animals in clothes on downtown
streets and where is everyone going? It's a short story
and a long story of greed in the face of Gandhi Yes
well that's pushing it but why is everybody rushing

around like bandits looking for a deal Why is this
guy on a street corner begging for a buck Why this
aged lady on another corner hawking flowers to save
herself And this funny fellow with buttons all over him
proclaiming the end of the world and nobody acting
like they notice as they rush by And it's a script for a
Pixar animated film in which every character is totally
motivated by what he wants And it's I want I want
but they don't say it Why say it when it's so obvious
Yeah all over America everybody is running around
intent on their own instant gratification and why not?
What else is there to live for I gotta get mine I wanna
I wanna I wanna Make a million overnight Git rich
quick & git out and have a mistress never mind the
global warming fuck all that I got to get to Fat City
and I mean soon Don't tell me Jim reaching for the
moon Just git out my way and fuck the nation of poor
assholes on the street I am an American I deserve
everything Me-Me-Me Nevermind what the scientists
are saying the human race might not make it to the
end of this here century but life goes on and on like a
roller coaster in an amusement park ZOOM ZOOM and
we're up and over and over

    MEMORY all gone into reveries the cherry time
over and what remains? oh I remain with Beckett and
Proust in the Amen Corner and will aureate dawn ever
come again? Will I survive will you survive even as
drones the size of hummingbirds can kill you or your

brother ten thousand miles away I shudder to think . . .
said the dame from South Side Boston but stopped
short without finishing her sentence as the light
dimmed in the Caffé Paradiso after they'd thrown out
Jack Powers black Irish and the last great poetry
spouter on the Near North Side Lord save us we all cry
together as if we all believed together that there was
such a thing as a God that metes out justice like
executing Whitey Bulger or whoever ran the mob and
there's no turning back when you do enough dumb
things to screw up the country and everybody knowing
what should be done but they don't do it and everybody
knows what shouldn't be done but they do it anyway
and bang goes the ball game and there ain't no joy in
Mudville even though there indeed are many
enlightened people on earth and I am tempted to say
that so-and-so living almost exclusively with animals
made her a truly enlightened being "Oh I must turn
and live with animals" said a famous poet and he did
he did oh are there not so many ways to live so many
ways to die and how many lives do each of us live in
one lifetime so many lives subsumed in one voice like
a flight of birds with a single consciousness and the
consciousness expressed in one cry in animals and in
one voice in man or woman as I myself lived more than
one life growing up yes and I'll get back to that if I live
long enough but for now I'm too busy living in here
and now in the vast marvel of being alive as part of

creation as part of the earth and sea and my blood is part of the sea And then there are the two fish swimming in tandem in one consciousness like the body and the mind vibrating together and unable to live without the other, the two fish of our body with one fate which is what that hatha yoga feller told me one day at the Tassajara Zen Center in Big Sur mountains Yeah he said Fix your mind and fix your body with my repair kit heal one and heal the other Yeah and if you believe that you'll believe anything without a computer Google or Wikipedia to tell you right or wrong and No you can't bring your iPhone into the yoga room You're on your own with only yourself and the hell with that house of cards the electronic universe which in an instant will collapse and disappear whenever the electricity goes off with a zizzle and a pop and you are left with nothing but yourself and no one to Twitter with Baby baby you've come a long way only to fall on your face with your Facebook and if you believe that you'll believe anything but you gotta believe in something Baby you gotta believe And ain't that the crisis of modern ape and especially the American North American variety with no myths of our own to believe in We landed here with the old European the old Greek myths the old myths like Christianity in our baggage and if we believe if we still believe all those fairy tales we'll believe anything which leaves us exactly where we are naked under the

apple tree with each other Oh so you think this is all
pop religion since I'm no enlightened being and who
am I to destroy your gods or whatever you live by? Well,
I won't argue with that, I've got other fires to start with
other fish to fry as for instance can anyone imagine
what the world would be like if life on earth reaches a
condition in which there would be no further need for
the left to continually dissent, when there would be no
further need to dissent And one swallow does not
make a spring but two swallows winging together with
one consciousness make a full summer so that if
enough people could wing together with one
consciousness—and that consciousness being truly
enlightened—would we not then bring peace and social
justice to all the world? indeed indeed And is all that a
crock of merde? indeed indeed Shall we just persist in
our cynical stance our genial cynicism as heard up and
down the alleys of Silicon Valley or Wall Street yeah
yeah business as usual Don't give me all that Man oh
man and "When you're up to your neck in merde
there's nothing to do but sing" quoth Samuel Beckett
in one of his more optimistic moods and and "Let us
spray" said the skunks in church Oh man shall I go on
and what else can I do but go on Is there no end to it
the voiceless wailing while members of the Pussy Riot
go on wailing in jail in Mother Russia and are denied
parole by the paternalistic court in Saransk on the
grounds that they had not sufficiently repented their

obscene acts in the Mother Church What next are we
to be denied sacrament in Sacramento since we did not
do right with our do-do And what am I to think if I
don't toe the line and my toe-jam gets me in trouble for
offending the noses of the High-Ups and they may not
approve of the too-strong smell of the rot of civilization
and its discontents oh yes and the dark knight rises
also yes it's upon us the final darkest night brandishing
a carbon sword and shall the world as we know it just
simply come to an end but what do we know what our
end really is or could be Well it's just like our
government to keep common ignorant people from
getting their just desserts or even just main courses in
the food-stamp dining halls of the greatest nation on
earth where everybody eats plenty and all the cars look
new what with the auto industry pumping out a million
new cars a year and where are they to go except to your
nearest stoplight or parking lot or ten-lane freeway or
autobahn like in the goody Godard movie where the
traffic jam is so bad the people in the cars start
erecting tents and camping out along the highway
waiting for the end of the jam and it all grows into a
vast encampment which eventually turns into another
city and where do we go from here sitting here on the
thruway waiting for liberation from pathogenic
industrial civilization until it becomes time to actually
dismantle this civilization but somehow without
throwing out the baby with the bathwater ha-ha Aye

there's the rub-a-dub as I circumnavigate the world
looking for an angry truth or falsehood Oh I should
turn and live with animals like Rima in *Green
Mansions* in a dream of green oh no none of that
turning my back on the world as it exists in turbulent
cities groaning with machines yes I have seen the
expatriates in places like Oaxaca or Katmandu or Fiji
fiddling with their mustaches and kicking back like
natives but the slow rot of being disconnected from
their own culture invisibly sinks them into insomnia
and boredom their brains rotted away like overage
cheese with the mold that grows in lotuslands and
their eyes get a faraway look and that ain't for me I
have to stay connected with the whole hairy mess and
the glory of it or the vainglory of life as she is lived in
our America god bless our hairy souls the sun is at the
meridian and anything can happen while the
government is going into mushroom cultivation
growing mushrooms in the traditional manner you
know the way it is done You keep the mushrooms in
the dark and you feed them *merde* yessir that is how it
is done Just keep the people in the dark and you can
do anything and everything and you don't even need
the Supreme Court to help you like letting Big Money
rule in a new corporate fascism Oh boy and what's next
just set 'em up in the other alley where the bowling
pins are all lined up and all you have to do is knock
'em down and you're king of the mountain and not

even a nail of thought in the plank of stupidity can
stop you And ain't that the sum of it And so why am I
watching baseball to escape the pain or ecstasy of
existence and the Reds are beating the Yankees and
should I be happy It's all relative and life depends on
the simplest things to yield a crop of happiness as if it
were something you could harvest like corn or clover
Oh roll me over in the clover Do it again Do I feel pain
when a thousand innocents die in an air raid but you
know who at the same moment I am having an orgasm
as big as any imagined by Henry Miller that is Henry
Miller from Brooklyn all or most all of his writing is
inspired by the raised phallus or the raising phallus
and then when he gets to be so old that he cannot get it
up anymore and then what does that do to his writing
which may or may not be out of juice if you know what
I mean like as if it isn't the same problem with for
instance D. H. Lawrence who died at forty-five or
hereabouts and thus never had to experience the
fading of the phallus and who would ever know if his
phallus-based writing would ever suffer the same
wilted fate as Henry from Brooklyn Yeah Yeah and so
why not believe in a meaty interpretation of literature
or lit as they dub it in the universities since what is all
our writing about male or female if it is not based on
that life force rooted in the heart of desire or in that
nest of flesh from which all life springs Oh endless the
splendid life of the world Endless its lovely living and

breathing its lovely sentient beings seeing and hearing
feeling and thinking laughing and dancing sighing
and crying through endless afternoons endless nights
drinking and doping talking and singing with endless
lively conversations over endless cups of coffee in
literary cafés on rainy mornings Endless street movies
passing in cars and trams of desire on the endless
tracks of light And endless longhair dancing to airless
punk rock and airhead disco through Milky Way
midnights to the Paradisos of dawn talking and
smoking and thinking of everything endless at night
in the white of night the light of night Ah yes oh yes
the endless living and loving hating and loving kissing
and killing Endless the ticking breathing breeding
meat-wheel of life turning on and on through time
Endless life and endless death Endless air and endless
breath Endless worlds without end of days in autumn
capitals their avenues of leaves ablaze Endless dreams
and sleep unraveling the knitted sleeves of care the
labyrinths of thought the labyrêves of love the coils of
desire and longing myriad endgames of the unnamable
Endless the heavens on fire Endless universe spun out
World upon a mushroom pyre Endless the fire that
breathes in us tattooed fire-eaters dancing in plazas
swallowing flaming gasoline air Brave the beating
heart of flaming life its beating and pulsings and
flameouts Endless the open fields of the senses the
smell of lust and love the calling and calling of cats in

heat their scent of must of musk No end to the sound
of the making of love to the sound of bedsprings
creaking to the moan of lovers making it heard
through the wall at night No end to their groans of
ecstasy moans of the last lost climax the sound of
jukebox jumping the flow of jass and gyzm jived in
Paradiso And then the endless attempts to escape the
nausée of Sartre the bald hills of burned-out sensation
joie de vivre in despair boatloads of enlightenment
ships of merde afloat by Charon's moat, greeds
hysterias paranoias pollutions and perversions Endless
l'homme revolté in the anonymous face of death in the
tracks of the monster state Endless his anarchist
visions Endless his alienation Endless his alienated
poetry Gadfly of the state Bearer of Eros Endless the
sound of the life of man on earth his endless radio
broadcasts and TV transmissions newspapers rolling
off endless rolls on rotary presses the flow of his words
and images on endless typewriter ribbons and tapes
automatic writings and scrawlings endless *poèmes
dictés* by the unknown Endless the calling on or
dangling dick and then telephones to ends of earth the
waiting of lovers on station platforms the crying of
birds on hills and rooftops the cawing and cawing of
crows in the sky the myriad churning of crickets the
running seas the crying waters rising and falling on far
shingles the lapping of tides in the ides of autumn salt
kiss of creation No end to the sea bells tolling beyond

the dams and dykes of life and the calling and calling
of bells in empty churches and towers of time No end
to the calamitous enunciation of hairy holy man
Endless the ever-unwinding watch spring heart of the
world shimmering in time shining through space
Endless the tourist-boats through it *bateaux mouches*
in endless canals millions of windows aflame in sunset
the city burns with leftover light and red-light districts
rock and glow with endless porn and neon cocks and
vibrators vibrating endlessly in lonely topfloor rooms of
leaning houses Endless the munching on the meat-
sandwiches of lust the juicy steaks of love endless
dreams and orgasms fertility rites and rites of passage
and flights of fertile birds over rooftops and the
dropping of eggs in nests and wombs the tempts and
attempts of the flesh in furnished rooms of love where
sings the stricken dove No end to the birthing of
babies where love or lust has lain No end to the sweet
birth of consciousness No end to the bitter deaths of it
in vain No end no end to the withering of fur and fruit
and flesh so passing fair and the neon mermaids
singing each to each somewhere Endless the slight
variations of the utterly familiar the fires of youth the
embers of age the rage of the poet born again No end
no end to any and all creation in the mute dance of
molecules All is transmuted All is muted and all cries
out again again Endless the waiting for God and Godot
the absurd actions absurd plans and plays dilemmas

and delays Absurd the waiting without action for the
withering away of war and the withering away of the
state Insane the waiting without action for the insane
ending! Endless the wars of good and evil the flips of
fate the trips of hate endless nukes and faults all
failing-safe in endless chain reactions of the final flash
while the White Bicycles of protest still circle round it
For there will be an end to the dogfaced gods in
wingtip shoes in Gucci slippers in Texas boots and tin
hats in bunkers pressing buttons For there is no end to
the hopeful choices still to be chosen the dark minds
lighted the green giants of chance the fishhooks of
hope in the sloughs of despond the hills in the
distance the birds in the bush hidden streams of light
and unheard melodies sessions of sweet silent thought
stately pleasure domes decreed and the happy deaths of
the heart every day the cocks of clay the feet in
running shoes upon the quay And there is no end to
the doors of perception still to be opened and the jet
streams of light in the upper air of the spirit of man in
the outer space inside us Endless rubaiyats and endless
beatitudes endless shangri-las endless nirvanas sutras
and mantras satoris and sensaras Bodhiramas and
Boddhisatvas karmas and karmapas! Endless singing
Shivas dancing on the smoking wombs of ecstasy!
Shining! Transcendent! into the crystal night of time
in the endless silence of the soul in the long loud tale
of man in his endless sound and fury signifying

everything with his endless hallucinations adorations
annihilations illuminations erections and exhibitions
fascismo and machismo circuses of the soul astray
merrygorounds of the imagination coney island of the
mindless endless poem dictated by the uncollected
voice of the collective unconscious blear upon the
tracks of time! The dancing continues There is a sound
of revelry by night

    AND Ignorance hung on a blind crab clinging to
a net blinkered by centuries of darkness but if you
want sex don't go to Henry Miller don't go to Proust
try out *The Story of O* and you'll live longer with a
raised clitoris I mean what to do I know Is not love
what makes the world go round and round and yet no
one really knows anything about it except that it works
Oh Mother Teresa what is your secret Is the *Mona
Lisa* really winking at me at us as if a nod from her
meant eternal love Oh baby baby and the Man without
Shoulders who can't lift his weight in butterflies is
now in charge of the world And is there any reason to
watch the World Series on TV while this is going on as
if the fate of the world were on the Men with Shoulders
out there on the Field of Dreams as if a bases-loaded
home run could change the fate of the spinning world
spinning with a curveball or one-hundred-mile-an-hour
fastball to wipe out our enemies and save the world
from whatever Yeah play the "Star-Spangled Banner"
and sing about "bombs bursting in air" to show "our

flag was still there" Yeah Yeah ain't it the truth boo-
boo boo-boo who will save us from total obliteration
if not the Men with Big Shoulders carrying big bats
phalluses dominoes over all Oh exquisite corpus feet
of clay! but this is no *zibaldone* summarizing the
ultimate incoherence of life on earth as she is lived
by us but in that very incoherence we can discover
those happy errors or illusions that give life meaning,
for it is in the physical and instinctual, not in the
mental and rational, wherein complicity with illusion-
happiness lies—and so and so, take that you hairy old
philosopher in your cubicle and let us be off to the
lands of the living and breathing and loving! And yet
and yet it could be said that there will never be heroic
generous and sublime action, or high thoughts and
feelings, that are anything other than real and genuine
illusions, and whose price must fall as the empire of
reason increases Oh yes oh yes indeed how true, how
true! but the World Series is on TV and the Boys of
October are swinging their phalli bats and the lovely
blonds are laughing in the bandstands the lovely
blonds with perfect teeth are holding out their arms
to someone the sun is bright upon them one and all
fifty thousand humans on a sunny Sunday in Fenway
Park in Boston where the bums still sleep under the
linden trees in Boston Common Ah yes the greatest
generation so dubbed by a journalist speaking of
those born 1919 or thereabouts like John F Kennedy

and others like meself yes indeed what a group and
did they not fight the good war and did they not etc
etc Yes World War Two it was and they in the flower &
flour of manhood not to slight the ladies me lad like
on a sunny morn when I saw a fine one with her skin
like peaches and cream singing to herself in an open
window a voice so pure a lilting voice the voice of her
race when predatory capitalism hits the fan! Oh that
was a moment of light in the universe but then comes
the darkness as our country turned to a Stark Time of
Haves and Have-Nots in a fractured land while at the
same time astronomers are reporting that their Dark
Matter probe has detected absolutely Nothing.

AND was it Lyndon Johnson who said "Ah never
trust a man until I got his pecker in my pocket" oh
man Didn't he have the skeleton key to everything
right there when he put his finger on the pecker in the
pocket yeah for the Pecker is indeed the Fourth Person
Singular and the vagina is also a Person speaking out
and the Voice of the Vagina is heard throughout the
land in vagina monologues while where the pecker
heads go ye shall follow and look how it led to the ruin
of many a president and many a king Pecker rose and
made its irresistible demands and bang goes the egg
money Wow and Woe Woe! Woe!

SO I am a man of a certain age And old memory
all gone and twisted into reveries like Krapp recording
his Last Tape and I'll have none of that Let the

doomsayers be doomed and my mind warring with
everything Life & Death and the older one gets the
more the mind wars with All while I am trying to
discover the plot of my life and can't be bothered
trying to find the plot of life on earth and the only
part of my plot I have discovered so far is that I am
growing older by the split nanosecond night and day
and all grows and grows to its fruition my fruition and
even my nose grows when I'm asleep (the historic fact
of noses growing while everyone sleeps discovered by
the Russian poet Andrei Voznesensky and revealed
in a poem whereas it should have been published in
a scientific journal) and anyway I simply can't stop
growing up and over and I shall wear and I shall wear
the bottoms of my Levi's rolled and walk and walk
upon the beach and hear the mermaids singing each
to each whilst still I know those ladies with flippers
for legs are in fact still singing to me Ah yes *je me
souviens* and you were wearing high heels and sheer
stockings that day in Ojo Caliente and nothing then
to do but loudly sing *Gaudeamus Igitur* as if the
whole aim of life on earth were to find pure love and
me hiding in plain sight for all to see Oh blind man's
bluff . . .

　　AND so the end of all my traveling toward the sun
great god sun in charge of all And the isles of Greece
which I never reached, nor landed on, ah the isles of
Greece the isles of Greece the Delphic mysteries the

Golden Fleece The light upon the seat eternal The
horses of Achilles weeping for Achilles The loves of
Sappho in the night The songs and cries of Sappho
The Delphic prophecies The Eleusinian mysteries
The sound of revelry by night on Mount Olympus The
orgasmic cries of Dionysus The high breasts of Helen
The long fair hair of Helen Her darkened eyes The
longing eyes of Penelope Aie! Aie! Ulysse! And "Audiart
Audiart where thy bodice laces start." "There is none
like thee among the dancers." And then the cawing
of crows mixed with the cry of nightingales at the
Fountain of Castalia And then the anger of the gods
And then the dire prophecies The wailing of sibyls and
sirens The cries of the vestal virgins The cries of Icarus
falling from the sky The foundering of ships at sea The
cries of the blinded Cyclops in his cave And the sun the
setting sun over the isles of Greece And the sound of
axes in the wood in the sacred grove And the Golden
Bough unfound beyond us still The dancers gone
under the hill Ah let the Golden Age return before
all ages end And we must burn!

   AH "Memory Foam" which remembers too much
including dreaming for we remember snatches of
our dreams while we are returning to consciousness
yes snatches of our former or future lives, real or
imagined, and my head made of Memory Foam
remembering everything as for instance that time in
Avignon when a fair woman got off the local train her

arms full of *lavande* the lavender flower of Provence
that is in its glory everywhere in late summer and
it seemed she headed straight for me and offered
lavande and herself to me and it turned out that she
was an existential editor's wife getting away from
existentialism as far as possible but back in Paris she
embraced existentialism while embracing me that
is to say she used existential arguments to disabuse
me of my youthful romanticism and time flew by and
then one day she moved with her husband to teach
in a French colony and I never saw her again but
existentialism was still with me like that time I spied
Jean-Paul Sartre with Beauvoir in the Brasserie Lipp
in Saint-Germain and me living on sixty-five dollars a
month on the G.I. Bill and could never afford to even
sit down in the Brasserie Lipp and so what am I to do,
go right up and greet the great Sartre and the great
Beauvoir and join easily in their conversation as if I
had the slightest idea what they were talking about
Oh yeah sure *Bonsoir,* M'ssieur Sartre etc etc ha-ha
before he signals the waiter and I am evicted and I'm
back on the street heading for my hole-in-the-wall in
Montparnasse where a cold pot-au-feu awaits me for
dinner as I imagine Monsieur Sartre staring after
me thru those thick lenses which I always suspected
prevented him from seeing anything at all in the real
world ha-ha and me still a romantic in spite of it all
my Memory Foam full of romantic failures but enough

not-failures which kept my romantic self alive Ah me
the treasure hunt for love never ends and always begins
again and then when you find it again ain't it sweet as
apple pie made with spring apples and the sap rising in
your blood?

BUT now that I have heard everything that I have
to say about everything it is high time for a great
epiphany or for the Alpha Mom or the Alpha Dad to
appear and enlighten us as to why exactly we are here
on earth and what is our hidden destiny and so in the
beginning was the word and the word was Godot and
the world was coming to an end even in the beginning
every moment a new beginning and the way forward
is the way back and in order to arrive where you are
not you must go by a way you have never been and
oh nevermind those fine old phrases Let's get back
to the present where the world is coming to an end
for the millionth time but this time it's for real yes
sir I'm not giving you some Old Wives' Tales by Irish
washerwomen gossiping in the dusk while washing
their clothes in the River Liffey while night birds
twitter and far-off field mice twit

WHILE I'm now sitting near this guy who keeps
taking off his sweatshirt or sweater and turning it
inside out and putting it on again and then after a
while he takes it off again and turns it inside out and
puts it on again and what else have I got to do but
watch this guy doing the same thing for a couple of

hours while all the clean guys and dames on computers
are totally absorbed in their little handheld gadgets
and never a one casting even a glance at the guy
changing his sweater inside out as if he actually didn't
exist in their world at all and I am imagining maybe
several hundred thousand computer persons all over
the city totally entranced by the moving words and
images on their little gadgets can you imagine millions
of them a whole new zombie generation on earth
computing their lives in pixels or whatever they are
and the guy changing sweaters all the time like he's
trying to change his identity maybe and become like
the nice guys all around him but, no matter how many
times he does his act, he never changes and will always
be the outsider trying to get in even though he can
plainly see that all these guys and dames are obviously
not very happy doing what they're doing because of
a huge void in their lives when they are constantly
trying to fill by constant contact online with others
trying to fill their own vast void of loneliness on earth
in their own brave worlds and so they're meeting all
kinds of strangers online and even actually meeting
some of them in person and now and then actually
marrying one or two of them and the café fills anew
with them every day and every day there are the
outsiders changing their sweaters or their pants or
suits or sexes to become one of the Happy Many and
where will it all end with a nation of this new unnamed

twenty-first-century breed of humans oh boy am I so
totally demented in my later years that I see the whole
of existence with a totally jaundiced eye in which
everything is turning into the worst possible world in
the worst possible universe and when you are up to
your neck *in merde* is there truly nothing to do but
sing? Or laugh as I did when I read that Flaubert's wife
or Stendhal's wife complained in a letter to a bosom
friend that her husband's penis was too small or was
too large I forget but in any case you can imagine the
embarrassment of her bosom friend upon receiving
this complaint for as it happens she too etc etc And
all café sitters waiting for who knows what like Lady
Godiva to ride by on a white horse shedding her
underwear as she passes and causing universal joy
and the stock market zooming up up up while the
poor get poorer and the rich get filthy richer while I'm
still waiting with Godot and a little guy goes by in a
sampan hat pushing a stroller and here comes a small
band of Indios playing their bamboo flutes and beating
small drums as if they as if we were in the Andes and
I am wondering what's happening to my fair city It's a
flat earth now and we're all in the new electronic Flat
Earth Society and on a clear day you can see almost
forever.

AND every day in this grand little café of life I sit
waiting to see how our little civilization develops, not
to mention how our little consciousness might develop

(Oh what ecstasies, what despair!), and there's a sign
outside the café that says HAPPY HOUR EVERY DAY
4–7 It's only 10 a.m. and no one is Happy yet A thin
young mother enters pushing a stroller in which sits a
little fucker and you can tell he's plotting something.
She goes over to the cold drink cabinet and picks out
a diet soda and then of a sudden the little feller starts
laughing for no apparent reason. It's already Happy
Hour for him, if laughter is a sign of it. I decide to
join him and then someone in the back breaks a laugh
and then pretty soon everyone in the café is infected
with laughing happiness and they're all laughing their
heads off like as if a day of universal happiness had just
been declared but now just as suddenly the little brat
starts crying and the party is all over and no one feels
like joining him in his lament and the mother wheels
him out of the café in a hurry as if she had forgotten
what laughing happiness is, while in front of my local
post office three mailmen are talking Cantonese and
laughing and after I mail some stuff I join in laughing
my head off and of course they are totally surprised
since white White Ghosts don't usually know Chinese
and they have no idea who I am, but I am the universal
man and I know Cantonese the way I know which way
is Up the way I know all languages spoken or silent
and as such I know everything and nothing I am
your universal wise man and your universal fool I am
your wise guy from Brooklyn and I am your Buddhist

guru in a saffron robe with supreme knowledge as to
how to exist on earth and elsewhere even as I stand
laughing with the Cantonese postmen and a dog walks
by leading his master on a leash and the dog lets out
one loud bark as he passes the postmen who continue
talking and laughing as if the dog didn't exist and
the dog is of course baffled by the Cantonese speech
but also by the speech in English by other humans
who sound all the same to him They just sound like
other dogs going woof-woof or bow-wow which is all
very baffling since he and other dogs, and perhaps
all other animals except humans, have no memory of
their own individual pasts, not really "remembering"
anything such as when and where they were born,
and isn't that strange that maybe we humanoids are
the only animals who have historical memory of their
existence on earth or elsewhere and not one animal
expert has any memory of when for instance the
ancient Egyptians existed except perhaps cats, those
sphinxes, those mysterious anachronisms who may
or may not remember when they were deities to the
ancient Egyptians, for who can tell what's going on
in any cat's mind or psyche when they don't give us
any sign that they know or remember anything about
everything much less the sacred rituals of deified cats
by the River Nile a long time ago And we with all our
Prousts remembering everything and every little thing
with our omnivorous memories *retrouving* the past in

sessions of sweet silent thought, while I see faces in
the leaves of trees embedded in the masses of leaves,
and often I discern a face a profile a pair of eyes or a
protruding nose and those are never faces I know never
familiar faces family faces or anything like that These
are strangers' faces some as ancient as days But who
are they and where do they come from in most any tree
I come upon are they all mementos of all the people
who have ever lived on earth Are they Mother Earth's
memory set forth here to remind the living of all who
have passed this way or any way oh boy they are always
all silent though they shake with any wind shake their
heads so to speak but all remains silent except for a
certain rustling a certain light breathing as if about to
speak but never do although they may grimace or seem
to laugh or weep or cry out yet never do as if all the
secrets of earth are hoarded in those faces those heads
shaking or still and awaiting the next good or ill wind
to agitate them again to set them trembling with some
new news of earth and womban. As when for instance
when Him shows up more than thirty years before his
own death on a cross and when he grows up and Mary
Magdalene becomes his wife and bears his children
then the apostles and other Wise Guys get very upset
because it was supposed to be some sort of celibate
bad boys' club with no begetting of children and they
forthwith ran off with Mary's babes and nowhere were
they to be found in the Holy Land and so it went down

thru the centuries that Jesus was celibate and Mary
merely a camp follower or a prostitute as pictured
fifteen hundred years later in Renaissance paintings
with Mary Magdalene hanging onto Jesus's hand like a
cast-off fan of *Jesus Christ Superstar* whereas the truth
was that she was hanging onto Jesus and beseeching
him to give her back their children to bring back the
very fruits of her womb and hung-up Jesus paying her
no nevermind, ah men, Amen.

    AND so one day it's the song of the sad café all
around me with everyone on their portable universes
their handheld computers and nobody talking
to anyone else and after a while I can't stand the
deafening silence any longer and so I up and speak
to the solemn guy at the next table like I say "I can't
resist asking what book you are reading" and he hands
me the book and it's *Advanced Astrology* and we
exchange looks and I blurt out "Ya know the Greeks
made it all up you know it's all their fantasy spun out
in the stars" etc etc and the guy gives me a strange
look and grabs the book back, not that I was trying
to hold on to it or anything since I gave up astrology
about the same time I wet my pants for the first time
and anyway the café returned to its total silence with
everyone screwed to their little computers as if life
depended on them which in truth is the case if they sit
there long enough glued to the little robots directing
their lives etc etc yessir you don't need to know

anything anymore all you have to do is turn on your
robot machine and it will tell you anything you didn't
know like when was Troy destroyed and whose face was
it that sank a thousand ships etc etc anything that you
want to know at your fingertips ain't it the truth and
me just sitting there looking around at all the closed
silent faces none of whom could sink a thousand ships
like Helen of Troy who could have sunk the whole
fleet but all that was then and this is now and how
shall I escape this boatload of somnolent café sailors
on a cruise? Let me tell you a thing or two about the
spinning world before it spins off its axis. The world's
an ice cream melting down and we are tiny animals
sprinkled on it, little animals with brains yeah the only
animalcules that recognize themselves in mirrors and
go wow! And Pope Francis a pope with a brain, can you
imagine a pope with a brain *mamma mia* ain't it so
but even he with his direct connection to Heaven can't
tell us why we are here and what is it we are supposed
to be doing here on earth, oh we weren't set down
here to play tennis and kill each other on pro-football
fields or in kickboxing rings, we weren't set down here
or set up here to be bowled over by the roller-balls of
world wars oh no we must have some higher or lower
purpose than that but what could it be except 23andMe
yes me and all my progenitors for I have weathered the
storm all the storms I have beaten them all I am the
man I was there when Rome was built I was with Noah

in the Ark I was in the manger with an ass I am the
man and I was there I have seen the mass mess but I
am the victor of my own life I am the conqueror of it
my own mock hero yes and am the captain of my soul
ha-ha yes indeed and everything is just fine everything
is wonderful except our little tribe is headed for the
big falls, our little world is coming to the end of the
wick woe woe woe Yes right now is the beginning
of the end and you ain't seen the half of it yet no sir
the final crystal night is approaching and what are
you going to do about it except sit upon the ground
and weep and gnash your teeth and cry but don't do
that yet don't leave the theatre yet there's still a lot
to come still a lot to see as for instance Holy Smoke!
As we used to say Holy Smoke is arising around us
descending on us and all comes down to Holy Smoke
and all our life dissolved in it and you and me with it
Holy Holy Holy "tongue and teeth and asshole holy"
in the Amen Corner with us backed into it woe woe
alack so let us pray to each other finding ourselves up
shit creek without a paddle with the latest scientific
evidence proving we are all in the Sixth Extinction
yes there having been five other extinctions of life on
earth before our own and ours only a few hundred
thousand years old and already we are on the way out
what a story woe woe all is lost the ship is sinking
although nobody even notices a tale of sound and furry
animals about to perish feet first into the final zero

oblivion and Love and Hate the viruses that eat us up
like cannibals insatiable woe woe and we are the tragic
heroes of the Sixth Extinction and our fatal flaws are
Love and Hate and so *Ainsi soit-il* so be it baby baby
roll me over in the clover roll me over on the grill I'm
done on this side turn me over to eternity O father
Our father whose art's in heaven Hollow be thy name
Thy Kingdom come and gone Thy will will be undone
on earth as it isn't heaven in the throes of ecosystem
collapse or relapse don't call me I'll call you Be lazy Go
crazy Join the movement Don't take medicine Eat the
garden Ignore government Disband the military Join
the pacifists Discover anarchism Resist and Disobey!

AND so then what am I doing in Saint Stupid's
Parade? Would you call the First Church of the Last
Laugh to be an act of disobedience or just plain
inflammatory insults to the status quo and praising
instead the Stations of Stupidity and the Tomb of
Saint Stupid and the Statue of the Bare Butt and God's
Cock?! Oh you contribute to the martyrdom of the
bishop, make your own bare-ass parade? But Saint
Stupid is so stupid that he/she continues to have his
parades on April Fool's Day every year and who's to say
it doesn't change the world at all as it goes on spinning
around mindlessly or mindfully? Am I so stupid that
I don't recognize a true prophet when I see one? So
why should I want to go on living if the whole world
is so stupid? But Saint Stupid no doubt has an answer

to all my doubts as for instance "we have nothing to fear except fear ourselves!" And is this April Fool's Day going to go on forever even after the last parade has passed and we are forever the Fool in the Tarot pack or are we all the Hanged Man in the pack forever lost dangling in space? Or should we all join the newest school of Buddhism in America in which instead of Hinayana Buddhism we have the "cosmic oneness" of all phenomena expressed in the new Hahayana Buddhism which aims "to transcend the inexplicable nonsense of human existence" as articulated by Hahayana's chief guru Scoopa-do Nisker who hopes to die laughing after persuading us all to laugh our heads off too while all the while thinking of dying and every third thought is Death.

BUT I am not the Hanged Man in the Tarot pack hung out to dry and twisting in the wind, for I still feel like an all-seeing all-hearing observer of everything going on down here on this earth, and here's a couple with knapsacks near me, and he's reading a mag and she's got her head down on the table, seeming to sleep. What's happening in this moment of their lives? He goes to the counter and comes back with a glass of red wine. Silence descends in the café, Sunday mid-afternoon. She raises her head for a moment to face the world then puts it down again. She's Asian, he's white and probably American. He's reading *The New Yorker.* He must have a brain or is just pretending. Perhaps

they are just a happy couple, and she exhausted from
making love all night or all day, and so Now what?
Will the skies open and a golden horse appear to carry
them away to some undiscovered *paradiso*? Is their
destiny written in the dregs of their wine, here where
life once-upon-a-time went on so unterribly that we
could not write the Great Russian Novel? I think of
greeting the guy cheerfully and striking up a bright
conversation. But what is there to say to passing
strangers lost in their own worlds and looking at you
as if you came from Mars or were a character in *Star
Wars* or some other escape fiction? Oh who knows who
knows and who cares, and in the end I get up and go,
leaving them to their inscrutable destinies, for the
witching hour is upon us, and it is high time to save
this world from itself, high time to transform the world
into democratic open-society socialism, to share all
the world's wealth with all the Wretched of the Earth,
while still the only God for all beings is consciousness
itself.

   WHILE in my homely little neighborhood café,
a homely little neighborhood fly lights on my table.
This fly was once on the wall in a position to hear
everything said in the café. But he was totally bored
by the chatter and decided to fly down and light upon
bare heads and hear the murmuring of their minds.
But I could not hear what the fly heard with his inner
ear—our unspoken stream of consciousness.

*WHILE dreams too are part of our consciousness,
our shadow consciousness, our first life, dreamt before
leaving the womb, and it continues on after birth,
absorbed in our consciousness, so that it's my old
dream of always trying to reach back, to find that
place where I was born but then in actual life going
there and finding it . . . The birth certificate says 106
Saratoga Avenue Yonkers . . . I take the A train to
168th Street, transfer to the number 1, and continue on
the Elevated to Van Cortlandt Park, then catch a bus
north to South Yonkers. It's only a mile or more along
the west edge of the park to Carroll Avenue. I get off
here on the vague advice of the old black bus driver
who waves in the direction he thinks Saratoga Avenue
might be . . . And so uphill half a mile on foot past
blocks of dark brick apartment houses their better days
behind them. And there's the end of Saratoga Avenue
with a mom-and-pop grocery. An old white man comes
out carrying a quart in a paper sack. He looks through
me as if I were part of the street and had been there
forever (Perhaps I have) . . . I have no memory of
the house or its location. It is as if I am looking for
someone else's birthplace (Perhaps I am). I pick up
my pace, hurrying along maybe three short blocks to
106 where in a small back bedroom my brother heard
my first cry (it echoes now as if I myself had heard it).
The little house almost to the crest of the low hill, a
gabled wood-frame house, two stories with an attic,*

*detached from close-by houses, a yard with old cars
on one side, and a steep drop in back to a gully with
a few tall trees, great old barren oaks and elms—bare
ruined choirs! The house itself run down now. Asbestos
siding over the old wood. And a small screened-in front
porch. Inside the flimsy screen door there's a once-
handsome oak door with worn brass doorknob and
bevelled glass upon which gold-leaf numerals still show
106 (with half the 1 missing). Three doorbells (three
apartments now?). I ring them all with no answer. No
one in sight anywhere inside. No sign of life in nearby
houses. A kind of country slum but still a quiet family
neighborhood. Across the little street some Latinos with
boom box turned down are hanging out. I walk around
back by the old cars and the bare trees and look up at
the silent house, looking for that small back bedroom.
Kikiriki goes a bird, just once, like an echo of light. All
at once, an incredible overflowing feeling of happiness
surges up from nowhere. Born here! . . . some three
hundred yards north of the northwest corner of Van
Cortlandt Park. It must have been all country back
then. The kids must have played ball in this green park
with its worn diamond and its ancient rusted screen
behind the batter's box. I can hear the bat hit the ball
(perhaps pitched by Pop). And my brother running for
first base ended up in Baltimore forty years later . . .
Shouts and laughter tears and whispers fill the air.*
    OH I miss the Hudson, not far from where my

consciousness was born, the great Hudson of my
childhood, the Hudson my Mississippi, when I was
a stripling lad on a Sea Scout canoe trip in the fall
of that year, with the yellow-red leaves falling on the
coursing water, the great trees hanging over the water
by Saugerties and Coxsackie, and my stripling mind
far away, so that unthinking I lost my balance and
tumbled into the rushing cold water, to be rescued
by Sea Scout hands, and then sat shivering on a
riverbank, but I was Tom Sawyer and I was Huck Finn,
and I was Injun Joe, the falling leaves blown about
us in Indian autumn, and I now one of them, falling,
fallen into loam of dark

   BUT there are crystal moments in time, crystal
moments in all our lives, fleeting past, whether it's
sunlight on a face or fog in a fir tree, a flash, a moment
in time, yes, such as when I was three or four and
playing hide-and-seek with my Aunt Emilie somewhere
in France, and I crouched down behind a wicker sofa
on a porch in sunlight, and Tante Emilie calling
over and over *Lu-Lu-Lulu où est-tu?* or such as that
moment in Paris yesterday or long ago when I met
my Nadja, my new illusion to live by, looking like a
normal person, a normal woman, but as soon as she
opens her mouth you know she is special, and she has
a laugh sometimes as if she were perpetually surprised
by life and the absurdity of it. Imagine, good looking,
speaking what she calls her Hollywood French. I

imagine all the things I don't know about her, and I
know practically nothing, except that she reminded me
of my dear aunt Emilie when I was a child in France
with her in her cloche hat and her hair cut like Louise
Brooks, and I do remember how often when I was with
her alone or in company she would burst forth "Oh, *je
t'adore, je t'adore*" and me only three or four years old
and not realizing "I adore you" is what most everyone
longs to hear all his or her life, yes, *"Je t'adore"* is
enough for a lifetime of living and dying. And now
we are separately staying in the Hotel Esmerelda on
the Left Bank around a corner from Shakespeare &
Co. bookstore and Nadja has gone off somewhere,
who knows where, while I sit in the window of this
little old hotel which seems to be listing a little like
an old wooden ship at anchor, which of course it is,
with no elevator and a narrow winding staircase and
rooms not much wider than the French windows, and
so here I am indulging in the real fantasy that I am
still a young student in Paris, yes, and why not, won't
I come back another year and find Nadja still here,
crying or laughing or talking brightly, and is she not
a little like having a gentle wild animal in the house,
and she could go off in wild laughter most any time,
or talk crazily on any curious subject, and whoever
was with her might say "Can't you just make regular
conversation?" She is like the flight of a bird on the
wing, aware of the air about her, when I'm with her

my time seems to stand still, time is on the wing with
her, and I sometimes think we would never die as
long as we were in sight of each other, or die together
sometime tomorrow, and perhaps Proust has a name
for this strange effect when *les temps perdus* are never
lost, and those lost times just stay in a memory bank
and accumulate interest or lose interest, like a bank
account, and so it is with Nadja and me. She is an
enfant du Paradis, a bird of paradise in the topmost
balcony of the world, while I remain here on earth,
and I am still a student at the Sorbonne on the G.I.
Bill, 1947, a little long in the whiskers for a student,
though I remember a student with a long white beard
at an advanced age coming into the Salle Richelieu
to defend his thesis on Flaubert's wife who wrote
a woman friend complaining about her husband's
penis being too small, and our scholar claiming he
had the documentation to prove it, and also stating
that he knew for a fact that Madame Flaubert was "a
hot tomato." But this all a long way from the Hotel
Esmerelda where it's been raining lightly, but now the
sun bursts through over the Ile de France in which
Paris nestles like a grey dove, and Nadja has been
doing laundry and now appears in a long white dress
perhaps of calico, and floats out front to the little parc
of Saint Julien-le-Pauvre in midafternoon, and there is
a stillness in the air, as if the turning earth stood still,
a breathlessness, as sun floods down upon the park

benches where I now sit with Nadja, a stillness in the world enclosing us, with no need for words, for what is there to say anyway except that we are all here under the dreaming trees, faced only with ourselves.

AN ant crawls across a table, falls off of it, onto the cobblestones. A gardener in baggy pants shows up with a garden hose and attaches it, and magically water spouts up onto a wilted flower bed, and the hushed silence continues in this little enclave of life, as I imagine it is the silence of happiness, Nadja too engulfed in it. No shadows here, no chiaroscuro, just us in sunlight. Paris may explode, the world may explode, but not here, not here. Life goes on, and us with it, and there is no end of it, eternal creation, birthing and dying, dust into dust, as my fantasy dies, as this present fantasy fades, in this eternal moment, realizing that Nadja is in her own world, in her own illusion of the moment, and does not share my fantasy of here and now, and she was never my lover nor would ever be, and perhaps her consciousness was all chiaroscuro, all shadow, though with her you could never tell where shadows began or ended—a fleeting darkness sometime flashing across her face, as a shadow from a passing bird or a driven cloud, to vanish in an instant from her face Yet at other times she would be totally with you, as that late afternoon strolling through the Luxembourg Gardens, the late sun slanting through the high trees by the Fountain

of the Medicis, as then we are sitting by the long pool
in front of the classic statues that spout water into the
still pool, and we sit still on the wrought-iron chairs by
the still water, as small birds dip by, half in sun, half
in shade, under the tall trees, and the water dappled
with shadows of leaves, in the late afternoon of that
year, and she exclaiming "Oh, I'm never going to leave
here ever, I'm going to write everyone we're staying
forever!"

YES, forever, and Little Boy grown up dissident
romantic or romantic dissident has his youthful
vision of living forever, immortal as every youth is,
believing his own special identity would never, could
never, perish, yes, believing all that, in the face of
the unrushing fate of the whole human race which
scientists predict will very soon totally perish, in the
Sixth Extinction of life on this earth.

AND that is why the cries of birds now are not cries
of ecstasy but cries of despair.

ACKNOWLEDGMENTS

Thanks to Sterling Lord and Mauro Aprile Zanetti.